Love,
Kristen

Dr. Oz—
Thank you for helping
to fight HPV and
cervical cancer.

Kirk

LOVE, KRISTEN
ONE YOUNG WOMAN'S COURAGEOUS BATTLE AGAINST CANCER

iUniverse books may be ordered through booksellers or by contacting:

iUniverse
1663 Liberty Drive
Bloomington, IN 47403
www.iuniverse.com
1-800-Authors (1-800-288-4677)

ISBN: 978-1-4620-8393-0 (sc)
ISBN: 978-1-4620-8394-7 (ebk)

Biography / Autobiography / Women

Printed in the United States of America

iUniverse rev. date: 02/21/2012

Love, Kristen

One young woman's courageous
battle against cancer

iUniverse, Inc.
New York   Bloomington

Two of her favorites . . . flip-flops and her red Mustang

Kristen Forbes EVE Foundation, Inc.

www.kristeneve.org

kirkforbes@kristeneve.org

DONATE TO FIGHT HPV & CERVICAL CANCER

Thoughts

"Being in the hospital has allowed me to see how many friends I have in my life. Most people would realize that they have fewer friends than they thought. I now know I have more close friends than I ever imagined. God has blessed me!"

Kristen Forbes

"I remember getting a Christmas card from Kristen last year. I thought it was amazing that with all she was going through, she was thinking of me and others and taking the time to show us. Her fruit of the spirit was shining! It's made me a better person, and one who wants to show and tell people NOW I'm thinking of them, not later. I know Kristen always put other people first and not just when it was convenient."

Karen Hopkins

"Kristen was one of my most pleasant and favorite patients. She was very special to all of us. I can still smell the flowers she brought to me the last time she was in my office. Her radiant and warm smile and gallant fight against cancer remains an inspiration to all of us . . . . and an example to all."

Dr. F (Oncologist)

"During an interview our daughter talked about her job and volunteer work with Relay for Life and how Kristen's life had impacted her to encourage more young women in the prevention of cervical cancer."

Carolyn Mendell

"In my view, probably the most important contributions I made were during those early years, before we really believed we could actually start a vaccine trial with the HPV vaccine. Some of us had more faith than others that it could work, and admittedly I was skeptical. I think it was a lot of perseverance, stubbornness and passion on the part of people in my group, at Merck, and other many other institutions who really kept pushing until we got something that looked like it would work."

Dr. Brown.
HPV researcher

Kristen and her Dad during a special moment at Disney

Kirk Forbes, Kristen's father, the author of *Love, Kristen* wanted to share Kristen's story with all the women who have fought cancer or will one day have to face it. He wants everyone who walks this path to marvel at the miracles that happen along the way. Kirk is a commercial pilot who spent his time between flights working on her story. It was therapy for him and a mission for all women.

Kristen's toughness was reflected in her love of rugby

The whole family

She loved him like a son

For Jacob

Whom she loved
and treated as her own.

God so loved the world
that
He made people,
people
that could write of
their souls

—Kristen

Kristen's beloved sun, sand and palm tree in her own hand

Contents

Why

As with most parents, we wanted to protect our children, especially when they started going out with friends and dating. Our concerns, like any parent, ran the gamut including drinking, drugs, car safety and picking the right mate. The possibility of advanced cervical cancer never crossed our minds.

This year more than 11,000 women will be diagnosed with cervical cancer in the United States. Almost 4,000 will die of this disease. This is equivalent to the 9/11 tragedy every year. In spite of these figures, the National Cancer Institute determined through a survey that only 40% of American women have heard of the human papillomavirus (HPV) infection. Only 20% of them had heard of its link to cervical cancer.

There are more than one hundred different types of HPV, the majority of which are considered low risk and do not cause cervical cancer. High risk HPV types may cause cervical cell abnormalities or cancer. More than 70 percent of cervical cancer cases can be attributed to two types of the virus, HPV-16 and HPV-18, often referred to as high risk HPV Types. HPV is estimated to be the most common sexually transmitted infection in the United States.

Thankfully, researcher Dr. Darron Brown's dedication has led to a medical breakthrough. He developed the HPV vaccine which gives women an opportunity for protection against this horrible disease. It has been proven effective against the two most common cancer-causing strains of HPV and licensed for use in the United States. At this writing there are two HPV vaccines available. Gardasil has been approved for females ages 9-26 and males. Cervarix has been approved for females ages 9-26. These age groups could eventually be expanded to include all ages.

Pap smear screening can identify potentially precancerous cells. Treatment can prevent the development of cancer. In developed countries, the widespread use of cervical screening programs has reduced the incidence of invasive cervical cancer by 50% or more. Women should have Pap smear testing even after vaccination.

It is generally recommended that all females, who have had sex, seek regular Pap smear testing. Guidelines on frequency vary, from annually to every five years. Kristen had a Pap test only 18 months before being diagnosed with cancer. In her case, an annual test may have detected it early enough to have led to a different outcome. Any interval longer than a year could be critical for many women.

Best friend Chelsea, Best friend Jeff, Sister Megan & Brother Eric

Foreword

I started assembling this book as therapy for me to get through the grieving process. The more I got into the task at hand, the more I uncovered about my daughter and her illness. Suddenly, this project became a mission to not only tell Kristen's story but to tell it in a way that may guide other parents onto a path of protecting their daughters and helping to eradicate the world of cervical cancer.

Another purpose of writing this story is to give five-year-old Jacob, whom Kristen loved and treated as a son, something he can read when he is old enough to understand just what a "brave chick" Kristen was . . . . and how she loved and touched the lives of many in her twenty-three years.

The compassion and support of the doctors, nurses, medical staff, pharmacists, physical therapists, transporters and EMTs were unwavering throughout her illness. Everyone took part in Kristen's battle like supporting soldiers. They encouraged us, hugged us, cried with us, ate meals with us, celebrated the small victories with us and ultimately grieved with us. They were guardian angels in Kristen's year long journey and soldiers in her war. Many were there to share tears and laughter, a late-night movie or just hold her hand. Her brother Eric overcame his hospital discomfort for his sister. Her sister Megan spent most of her summer at home to be with Kristen. Best girlfriend Chelsea and best friend Jeff, along with his young son Jacob fulfilled the role of comforter and caregiver.

This book also gives me the means to publicly thank all of our family, church family, and friends beyond number who daily showed their concern through their emails, cards, text messages, letters, meals and generosity. Most importantly, we thank God for allowing us to have Kristen for twenty-three years.

Brenda and I hope that this book might offer comfort, hope and counsel to those patients, parents and caregivers fighting cancer.

Kristen, especially in her final year, touched countless lives. We can never thank her enough.

Kirk Forbes

Author and Father

January 2009

Email: piplance@aol.com

Such words
that are so unexpressed
will this last
or is it just a simple test

—Kristen

The Girl

Kristen grew up in a normal family environment, being the middle child of three including her brother Eric and sister Megan. Kristen was a good student and had above average grades at Noblesville High School. Her creative writings, especially her poetry and songs, were hidden from her father until now. Kristen was multi-talented, playing both the cello and guitar while participating in the high school orchestra. She played rugby (football without pads) only after working hard to convince her Dad "it wouldn't do her in." Her greatest accomplishment was graduating from one of the top business schools in the country, Indiana University Kelley School of Business. In May 2007, Kristen graduated with a Bachelor of Science Degree in Business and dual majors of Management and Human Resource Management. Her peers thought very highly of her.

She was always organized, focused on the task at hand and, like her father, always worked off of a to-do list. This discipline allowed her to hold down management jobs while carrying a full class load. Her employers said she was an exemplary employee and very hard worker. During high school and college she helped to manage a gourmet pizza restaurant and a custard stand. She also filled in as a substitute elementary teacher and a summer camp counselor for the YMCA. She was a lifelong member of the Girl Scouts, Day Camp Aide and traveled with them to one of their World Centers, Pax Lodge in England. When interviewed for an internship and management training position at Walgreens, the recruiter reviewing her resume asked, "How in the world did you hold down two jobs and still go to college full time?" After college graduation, Kristen became an Assistant Manager at Walgreens.

Kristen loved animals, including four German Shepherds she grew up with—all named Duchesse. Her two kittens, OJ and Fiji, helped keep her spirits up during her illness. On vacation trips to Florida she would stand watch for manatee and dolphin. She was especially fond of Key West. Kristen loved wearing her flip flops on the beach while enjoying her favorites . . . sun, sand and palm trees. She was a big fan of Jimmy Buffet, and made it a point to have a cheeseburger in paradise at Margaritaville on every visit. Florida also offered two other special places for Kristen, Disney World and SeaWorld. Her dreams included moving to Florida and opening her own restaurant, one that had menus made entirely of pictures.

Kristen had a deep compassion for her friends. Sometimes it got her into relationship problems, not knowing when to exercise tough love with some of her friends who needed it. She had a strong Christian faith and frequently helped her friends understand God's love and forgiveness. She went on several mission trips and participated in Emmanuel United Methodist Church's Youth Group.

It was the simple things that brought Kristen the most joy. She loved relaxing with a book, watching a movie with friends, driving her Mustang, scrapbooking, drawing, coloring, sipping chocolate milk, listening to Jimmy Buffet and the Dave Matthews Band, eating Mexican candy and spending time with Jacob.

Her greatest attributes were her ability to love everyone and her strength of character. Even when things were not going well, she never lost faith. She had a great sense of humor and a wonderful laugh. Her quick wit always produced good one-liners. She looked forward to seeing her brother Eric get married, help him pick out the engagement ring and be in his wedding. She wanted to be healthy again, marry and have a family of her own.

Kristen was very special. Her brother Eric said, "She always gave me a hard time when I didn't want to do something that could possibly bring me out of my comfort zone. — She always had a way of making me feel comfortable. — She was always there for me".

And her best friend Jeff said, "There was something about her presence that put me completely at peace".

No one would disagree.

Her greatest achievement was graduating from a top business school

I love making decisions
on my own
my thoughts
my soul
things work out the way
they should
unless time
becomes mixed up
thrown upside down
relief is coming countdown
Sun rises and nose is
still in the books

—Kristen

With the girl cousins

You can't survive when you're lonely
or with low self esteem
walking around looking for the
wrong thing doesn't help
love everyone
and let them know
faith helps us hold on
love keeps us going
find someone and give them
some sunshine
we all need a little
nothing matters until
mattering means nothing
want what you have
wishing gets you nowhere
things that happen today might
not be here tomorrow so
enjoy it
and celebrate

—Kristen

Diagnosis

None of us, Dad, Mom, Megan, Kristen or Eric had ever experienced a serious illness, injury or hospitalization before this. It was a new experience for all of us. This type of battle consumes everyone's life . . . including caregivers. Everything else gets put on hold. Every waking moment we were focused on Kristen . . . her illness, treatment, medications, and future. We learned how important the internet is . . . not only with researching drugs and treatments but solace and prayers from a very large support group of literally hundreds all over the globe.

A month after graduating from college, June 2007, Kristen noticed her right ankle was starting to swell for no apparent reason. Kristen started a journal to record her health problem and its treatment. Her own words tell her story best. In addition, when the problem became paramount for her mother and me, we enlisted help from family and friends by sending update emails. I have included these to tell Kristen's complete story.

* * * *

Kristen's Swollen Leg Journal

June 16, 2007—Saturday

Swollen ankle (right)

June 17—Sunday

Whole swollen right leg
Emergency room visit
Ultrasound on right leg—showed no blood clots

<u>June 20—Wednesday</u>

Appointment with Dr. L my primary care physician
Told to wear hose while at work, otherwise wrap it, Ibuprofen and ice
Check back within a week if it doesn't get better

<u>June 29—Friday</u>

2:15 pm doctor appointment with Dr. L
Right leg measured 2 inches larger
Sent to Riverview Hospital for another ultrasound (nothing reported)
CT scan (nothing) (1)

<u>July 5—Thursday</u>

4pm Doctor appointment

*   *   *   *

The Ultrasound revealed reduced blood flow back to the heart from her foot (obstruction in the vein?). After the Ultrasound was done, the technician had a very concerned look; walked down the hall with us and told us good luck . . . . but didn't say what she saw. I had a bad feeling about this.
Dad

<u>July 10—Tuesday</u>

Doctor appointment to go over all of the results of the tests
2nd ultrasound, blood flow going back up leg seemed to be sluggish
MRI (2) showed fluid in pelvic area
Right ovary larger than the left
It also seemed the right ovary was sitting on top of my leg muscle

<u>July 12—Thursday</u>

10 am OBGYN Appointment with Dr. N
No way any scar tissue, possible cyst on right ovary. She felt both ovaries, determined the right was slightly larger. Appointment for ultrasound set.
1:30pm vascular surgeon determined that I have a blood clot in my pelvis

<u>July 13—Friday</u>

Dr. L called and left a message saying go to the hospital. Talked to Dr. U and he said I was a direct admit.
Put in Pediatrics ward and was given the room phone number to the jail instead of my actual room.
Put on a slow drip of a blood thinner Heparin level at 30 needed to be up to 80.

*   *   *   *

Daughter Kristen is being admitted to Riverview Hospital in Noblesville tonight. She has suffered leg swelling for about three weeks and has been to four doctors, had X-ray, CT scan, MRI and Ultrasounds. The last doctor, a vascular specialist, said blood clot. They are putting her on an IV of Heparin (anti-coagulant).

Prayers requested.

Thanks,
Dad

<u>July 14—Saturday</u>

Taking blood pressure, temp and pulse every 4 hours
Drawing blood every 6 hours to check protein level.
Testing urine, took 16 vials of blood for tests.

*   *   *   *

Kristen is having 16 vials of blood drawn as I type. The Hematology specialist is going to check everything. She is on bed rest only until they can confirm dissolving of the blood clot. My guess is 4 days to a week. We will see. She has high spirits and is glad they finally found the problem.
Mom

<u>July 15—Sunday</u>

4 hours blood pressure, pulse, temp
6 hours drawing blood
CT scan to check on the clot

Results reviewed and ordered a chest X-ray which showed nothing
Also ordered internal ultrasound
Taken off the Heparin IV drip
Put on Coumadin
2 shots daily of Lovenox
Iron IV once a day
Iron supplement 2x a day
Stool softener once a day

July 15—Sunday

God is good and the doctors are making progress. Her blood chemistry numbers are coming into line regarding the Heparin's anti clot mechanism. They are still concerned about trying to figure out what caused a clot in a young, healthy adult . . . very rare.

July 16—Monday

New doctor came in at 6:15 am, a friend of the blood doctor said he wanted to do a CT scan of my chest.
Told me I would be here a few more days.
Nurses came in 6:50 am, told them about my cramps and migraine problem. She said she'd check with pharmacist for pain medicine.
Decided she would get a Dietitian to explain my new diet.
I'll be taking the iron IV the next 10 days.
Dr. U said he wanted the chest CT scan but was putting the CT scan of my belly on hold because I've already had one and he didn't want me exposed to that much radiation.
Went down to get internal ultrasound—waiting for doctors to give results.
Been nauseated all morning took anti-nausea medication and it worked for the most part.
I think what's left over is from being hungry and nervous. Dad is coming home around 9 pm.
Dawn, a dietician, came and talked to me about ways to increase iron.
Pharmacist is supposed to talk to me about the blood thinner.
Dr. D explained that Coumadin would not allow the clot to dissolve with treatment. Aggressive treatment would involve a catheter (with a filter) to allow enzymes to dissolve the clot or just allow the thinner to naturally dissolve the clot. Permanent chronic swelling would /could

occur if they allow the thinner to naturally dissolve the clot, so they (all Doctors involved) would get together and weigh the pros and cons to each simulation . . . So the Saga continues.

A pharmacist came to visit. Through her I discovered it's the iron that makes me sick
CT scan negative

Gynecological Oncologist

Mass in pelvis
Large
Infection, abscess, tumor

Surgical procedure to see what it is.

My stomach is going crazy! I'm so nervous about getting an IV and then Iodine for the CT scan. Last night I slept 4 hours and possibly another 30 mins. It was a long/short day. It's now 11 pm and so I basically can't understand how I'm not asleep. My Dr. is back tomorrow and I know she'll be explaining a lot of things (everything).

Sister Megan came up from Florida.

Brother Eric came to visit and I know that was hard for him. He told me the last time he saw Grandma she was in a hospital bed and throwing up. So I shared my story with him. It was a moment.

I want to know why my body is so screwed up. I want to know all the results from these tests and I want to fix my body.

I have many people praying for me, I can feel it. I can also feel my body getting much worse.

I'm scared!

<u>July 16—Monday</u>

Transfer from Riverview Hospital to Indpls. St. Vincent's Hospital

As the EMT's were loading Kristen in the ambulance we took photos. The EMTs must have thought we were nuts, they have never had anyone do that. Kristen waved and smiled for the camera as her gurney was put in the ambulance. In retrospect . . . I wonder if everyone at Riverview Hospital knew how serious this was . . . . except us?

We followed the ambulance to St. Vincent's Hospital and went up to the 6th floor. My heart sank as we rolled from the elevator to 6th floor south . . . . went under a corridor sign that read Oncology floor. The potential reality was now sinking in. Everything inside me tightened up. None of us discussed it but I felt like we were on a train going wherever it was headed with no say as to its destination.

July 17—Tuesday

We are setting in the lounge at St V's. The doctor did a pelvic exam on Kristen and found "abnormalities". They think the mass is related to the "abnormalities". She is going to have another CT scan at 7pm. Not only does she get the injection of iodine, she is drinking a liquid that makes everything glow. They are going to do a biopsy. Because of the drugs she has been on, they will have to put her under. Thank you all for your continued prayers. We can't thank you enough.

July 17—Tuesday

Yesterday, Dr. U and Dr. L came in and informed me that I have a large mass by my right ovary. They sent me to St. Vincent Hospital so a Gyn-oncologist can take a look. Dr. F (Oncologist) called and informed me why he made this move. He wants a surgeon to take a look and see what it is. The VP Nursing and the CEO of the hospital came to visit me.

Today the Tylenol didn't make the pain go away so nurse H called Dr. L and she suggested morphine which did nothing. So my new nurse J gave me Vicodin and the pain went away but I definitely feel a little weird!

Earlier I asked Dad, Mom and Meg to go check the hospital out because I needed some space. Damn I am out of it.

Baseball size . . . if cancer . . . . kidney function

Endometriosis can form masses

20

Cancer—increase chance of clots

Blood work . . . cancer tumor markers that are more common
Pelvic exam

Review records and options for surgery
Dr. D (Gyn-Oncology Surgeon) looked internally
Cervix is abnormal, possibly a growth . . . ordered another test

If they stop the blood thinner a clot could move, need to resume in 24-48 hours
Next week . . . blood filter placed . . . biopsy . . . blood thinner
After surgery start thinners and wean off shots
Wait for biopsy 1-3 days

July 18—Wednesday

Got about three hours sleep
Biopsy at 5 pm results could show cervical cancer
Passed out afterwards
Had blood filter placed in me about 9 am
No pain
Dr. D—examination under anesthetic
D & C Procedure (3)—check uterus with a camera, maybe take some tissue
And biopsy the mass

Take me
break me
prepare me Lord
For my life is yours
fill me
with your
Holy Spirit
Be kind to others you say
Late at night
I close my eyes to think of you
distractions will come tomorrow
I'm not ready for them
nor anything else

—Kristen

July 18—Wednesday

After biopsy surgery we all gathered together (except Kristen, who was sleeping a lot, recovering from the surgery) and were told that it was confirmed advanced cervical cancer. We all cried. It was expected but still a horrible shock. Kristen was told the next day. She cried and asked us to leave the room so she could cry alone and absorb the diagnosis. We went downstairs and stepped outside into the warm July afternoon and everyone had a major meltdown. Then Kristen sent us a text message for us to come back. The nursing staff was wonderful. Dr. F (Oncologist) took charge at this point.

I stepped into the hallway to talk to Dr. F and he asked how Brenda and I were doing. I told him we were praying for a healing miracle. Dr. F said we need to watch for the miracles along the way. He was right . . . . we were about to embark on a tough but amazing journey.

July 19—Thursday

It's cervical cancer
MRI and PET scan (4)
Everyone was told last night but me, of course.

Chemo . . . Radiation . . . . Surgery . . . . Radiation . . . . Scan . . . and come up with a plan

Keep from spreading

Call re benefits at Walgreens

PET scan Monday 3pm
MRI today . . . got copy of scan
Meeting with Radiation Oncologist Dr. H

Nurse E with Radiation
4-6 weeks daily treatment
Sounds like X-Ray

Side effects
Fatigue—more like flu, listen to my body
Week 3-4
Skin reaction pink or dark red

Itchy/tender to touch
Increase discharge, pain, bleeding
Bladder issues / diarrhea
25-30 treatments
Then inside radiation treatments
Next steps
Treatment planning CT scan
3-7 days put radiation landmarks on—take care of area, don't wash, mild soap and pat dry
Moisturizer on lower abdomen after treatment and before bed
Can work with appointments need to be at same time every time 4-6 weeks until checked for treatment

Dr. H (Radiology Oncologist)

Radiation and Chemo best eradication
Work together
Tired gradually
May urinate / bowel movement more frequently

Chemo . . . injection Cisplatin
After 5 weeks have an operation
Insert pen size tubes into uterus . . . then put in radioactive pellets
2 weekends in a row
Hospital stay for a few days

After few weeks repeat exams

* * * *

Our friend Bill was with us when the doctor told our family that Kristen had cancer. After Kristen was told the diagnosis, Bill decided to share his cancer story with her. Several years ago, Bill was diagnosed with terminal cancer. He told Kristen that the doctors held out little hope for his survival. However, God had a different idea and saved his life. He is living proof that God does work miracles because he should not be alive today.

Suddenly our lives changed. Everything else came to a screeching halt. Our schedules became Kristen's medical schedule. We were consumed by and focused on the battle about to begin. Now our lives consisted of setting schedules for treatments, appointments, tests, and research on the Internet to understand this disease and its treatment.

July 20—Friday

Hebrews 9:6-7

(When everything had been arranged like this, the priests entered regularly into the outer room to carry on their ministry. But only the high priest entered the inner room, and that only once a year, and never without blood, which he offered for himself and for the sins the people had committed in ignorance).

Permission to go outside?

3 ways of treatment

1. Investigational
    Chemo first
    Radiation
    Clinical Trial

2. Radiation and Chemo . . . . Standard

3. Start with surgery and remove as much of the growth as possible

    CT scan 3 weeks after 4 weeks of Chemo/Radiation treatment

Dr. F (Oncologist) came and talked with me, asked how I was emotionally, told me that they will need to get together and plan out my treatment.
Dr. D (Gyn-Oncology Surgeon) came afterwards and talked to me about 3 different options of treatment and looks like I'll be having surgery early next week.
I have permission to go outside 30 mins at a time. I've been in the hospital for a week and the only time I've been outside was when I was transferred from Riverview Hospital. Yea!!

10:00 am

I'm sitting here at St. Vincent Hospital in the Oncology wing, 6th floor, by the window. I checked into Riverview Hospital last Friday. It's amazing it's been a week. Found out yesterday that I have cervical cancer and that because of treatment my body won't be able to carry a full term pregnancy. Can you believe that? Dr. E is suppose to come talk to me sometime today about my options of saving eggs and all that fun stuff.

10:30 am Citrucel vs. Metamucil . . . Citrucel is not as gas producing

D with Dr. H (Radiology Oncologist), the lady that will be doing most of my treatment. Told me my internal radiation treatment will happen 4 weeks after my CT scan

10:50 am B—the social worker from the support center visit

2:00 pm Dr. H (Radiology Oncologist)

Stopped by and shared his personal story of him and his wife not being able to have kids. He adopted two kids and shared how wonderful it is. It's so nice to have doctors like this! It's wonderful to know that I have doctors that care for more than just my health. Dr. H doesn't even work over in the hospital but on Thursdays.

Last night Chelsea and I needed a Bible and asked L, my nurse, if she had one. She said probably and then returned later with another patient's Bible because he was allowing us to borrow it. Today my nurse, M, brought in this huge blue Bible for me. This was a Bible bought for me. This is what I believe you would call "seeing God". It's beautiful to know and have such wonderful people surrounding me.

July 20 5:46 pm—Friday

She has wonderful care and we are very impressed with the doctors. Kristen has a journal with all of her tests and meetings with them. She was supposed to have a CT scan today, but it was postponed. She has a PET scan on Monday. We just finished talking with her Gynecological Oncologist. Since Kristen was sleeping, he said he would see her in the morning. They are working as a team of doctors and will have a case meeting. Option A is radiation, B is radiation and chemo and C is surgery. He talked more about surgery with Kristen this morning, but now is thinking Option B is the best way to go. She is constantly coloring in coloring books and has her artwork on the bulletin boards in her room. Her creativity is really coming out. She has dedicated her drawings and given them to the doctors and nurses. She is really winning the hearts of the medical staff.

She is very anemic and gets a bag of iron plus two iron tablets every day. The iron makes her nauseated and she takes a pill for that. Additionally, she is taking a pain pill now. She is still feeling the effects of the biopsy procedure. The tumor is the size of a softball. We are not sure if it is a mass or a lymph node. The lymph node is a common place for this cancer to appear.

We are in a whirlwind, just taking it a day at a time. One never knows what tomorrow is going to bring.

We talked with the radiation doctor yesterday. When he said it would put Kristen in early menopause, she lost it. He was so good with her. He stopped, put his hand on her leg and let her cry, apologized to her profusely, since he thought she already knew. Later it was just her and I. We hugged and cried. She said I don't know why I am going through this, but I do know that God has a plan for me. She kept crying and finally she said in a clear non-crying voice "Move Mom!" The nurse was behind me with her pain pill.

Kristen's friend Meghan H works in the ER (Emergency Room). She heard Kristen had been hospitalized and came up and saw her last night. During this lengthy hospital stay, Kristen earned the nickname of "Princess". It was so appropriate because everywhere in the hospital she went . . . surgery, radiation, imaging, etc. , she had an entire entourage tagging along behind her . . . Mom, Dad, Sister, Brother, friends. Meghan H noticed this transformation. She surprised us all one night and delivered Princess Kristen a tiara with matching earrings.

Our daughter Megan drove up from Florida last weekend to help care for her sister.

Mom

July 21 Saturday

Dr. D (Gyn-Oncology Surgeon) stopped to re-emphasis the choices of treatment. He told Meg and I what Dad asked him "What would you do if it was your daughter?"

Had lots of visitors!

*　　*　　*　　*

When Dr. D (Gyn-Oncology Surgeon) told all of us it was cervical cancer the whole room came apart sobbing and crying. I wondered (and told him so later) how he could go home an hour later and eat a normal supper with his wife, son, and daughter after giving us that crushing news and participating in the meltdown that followed. I told him he had a special calling and that we all appreciated the huge sacrifice and mental anguish borne by him. I know that being the news giver must have been a major burden to carry. He really appreciated the compliment and almost cried. I don't know how they do it and still carry on normal family lives. We no longer saw Dr. D as a doctor but as a member of the family. We invited him to bring his kids out and go fishing off our dock. Dr. D said he could see our strength and faith in our example and email updates. It allowed people to pray for us without feeling they were "bothering" or interrupting us. We were always looking for the miracles.

We found out later that after Dr. H prematurely told Kristen she would not be able to have children he went back to his office and cried.

God bless all the doctors and their families . . . they are very special.

July 21—Saturday

The PET scan will reveal if the cancer has spread to other parts of the body. The chemo/radiation combo treatment hopefully will kill the large mass. The future will depend on how effective this five week treatment is. First, she will have Cisplatin chemo with external beam radiation followed by two rounds of internal radiation by implanting radioactive seeds near the mass. All we can do is hope for the best, and take it one day at a time.

I met with Dr. D yesterday. He laid out the possible routes: 1. chemo only 2. radiation 3. combo 4. major surgery. They first leaned toward major surgery then the combo program. I looked him in the eyes and said "Doctor, if this was your daughter what would you do?" His immediate response was, "Let me think about it . . . that is a fair question". So I said, "Ok, go home, have a nice restful weekend and think about it. Then come back Monday with an answer". He agreed.

I plan to write a letter to the hospital CEOs of St. V's and Riverview telling them how impressed I am with the knowledge, skill and compassion of their staff. The technology is incredible (can you tell I haven't spent much time in hospitals . . . thankfully). Dr. F, the Oncologist, has experience from Johns-Hopkins, Dr. D, the Gyn-Oncology Surgeon, trained at Brigham Women's Hospital—Harvard Med School, and his assistant doctor is from Ohio State. All the nurses were trained at Purdue, Indiana State and Indiana University . . . yea! They have been incredible too.

Kristen's spirits are fantastic . . . she has kept her sense of humor . . . has been coloring pictures and hanging her art on the walls. She has named her blood filter, Wilbur . . . her mass Cletus and her cervical cancer Wally. She is a bright shining star on a hallway, that gets bad news on a daily basis. Frequently when I step out in the hallway, I see someone standing or hugging while sobbing and crying because someone they love has just been given tough news.

I knew we were in trouble when Dr. F filled out the FMLA (Family Medical Leave of Absence) forms for me. He answered the question "how long do you expect this condition to require leave for this employee?" . . . he wrote six months. In addition, no one ever mentioned a hysterectomy which meant they were not concerned about taking anything out . . . . not good! Dr. F had even brought up the possibility of putting Kristen into a clinical trial . . . . ouch! The stress levels continue to rise.

July 22 Sunday

Felt like crap from gas and constipation. Dad rubbing my back makes me feel much better. Dr. E came to visit to deliver the news of there being no chance really to save any eggs. That's ok. I know that all of this is in God's hands. I read the Bible last night and it felt good . . . made the pain in all parts of my body subside!

*   *   *   *

We ask for your prayers tomorrow that the PET scan will show nothing anywhere else in Kristen. It is scheduled for 3 pm. Also for the major decisions that need to be made as we move forward on her treatment and the route that is the best way to attack this cancer, or as she calls it Wally and the mass Cletus.

Thank you so much for all your prayers through this trial. We were so blessed today by our wonderful church family. Bill delivered a card with cash to help us cover meals and gas. What a generous group Emmanuel United Methodist Church is. Then we get home and an angel had mown our yard!

Because of concern of a blood clot not dissolving and moving into her lung, they installed a blood filter in her vena cava to protect her heart and lungs. When they wheeled Kristen back from the blood filter installation, she was sitting up on the gurney, smiling, and holding a huge manila envelope. She proudly announced that it was the X-ray image of the blood filter she had named Wilbur. I laughed and taped the X-ray film up on her window so she could show all her visitors and tell her story about Wilbur.

<u>July 23 Monday</u>

Dr. F (Oncologist) stopped in this morning. My chemo and radiation is going to be done in Fishers right next to my apartment. So I am going to be doing another 6 months in my apartment.

Dr. D came in, I have surgery scheduled tomorrow at 2:30 pm. I have to stop eating and drinking at midnight. My PET scan today is at 3 pm. I had to stop eating at 11 am. When I get back they are going to be putting me on IV fluids. Yea! My digestive system seems to be working a lot better today. Dr. D hung out with Dad and me for about an hour. He is a wonderful man and Dr. F gave me a hug. If all goes well, sounds like I'll be leaving Friday and starting treatments about 10 days after surgery.

Being in the hospital has allowed me to see how many friends I have in my life. Most people would realize that they have fewer friends than they thought. I now know I have more close friends than I ever imagined. God has blessed me!

I went outside today and it was beautiful. I almost forgot it was summer outside; we took a shuttle outside to the Oncology Center where Megan, Mom, Dad and I hung out at a picnic bench. I noticed Gary's (Dad's friend) work trailer, so Mom yelled over at him and he came over and visited for a few minutes. With the PET scan I had to lay still for 1 ½ hr before the 30 min. scan.

We ate Fazolis. Chelsea came to visit as well as Eric and Jamie. My favorite Nurse L is back tonight but at the other end of the hallway. She came and said hello.

Megan also is staying with me and I just recalled the cheesecake in the fridge and I have until midnight to eat.

*   *   *   *

I love my sister, could never tell her how much I appreciate her support and love. Plus she keeps me updated on what Mom really thinks.

I enjoy when it rains early in the morning
nature sleeps in
to be like nature
free as the wind
maybe it should rain on someone
else's day not
this life
wishing days would pass by
but how hopeless
wishing life away
enjoyment
something someone may dream to enjoy

—Kristen

The Battle Begins

<u>July 24—Tuesday</u>

I researched online and found it was Stage 3C out of 4 stages. The NCI website (www.cancer.gov) is the best source of cancer related information, especially if you read the doctor's side in lieu of the patient's side. My heart sank when I read that statistically she had a survival probability of 30% after 3 years. Then my mind reasoned that if you are the one that survives then survival is 100%.

Please pray that it hasn't spread or it will be like getting hit by a truck a second time. Monday evening the doctors will conference and map out a treatment plan. Monday, Dr. D and I went into the Oncology floor family lounge and sat down at the table. He said he thought about it all weekend and said he would tell his daughter to do surgery. He then went to Kristen and told her. Kristen at this point had built confidence in Dr. D and his concern for her. Dr. A his resident (assistant) doctor was very concerned about Kristen too.

Surgery is over. They took out two lymph nodes but had to leave the large softball size mass in because it had grown into the vein and muscle tissue. Trying to remove it would have put Kristen at serious risk.

So the plan now is to let her recover 7-10 days then do a radiation/chemo combo therapy. PET scan showed no cancer outside pelvic area . . . fantastic news.

<u>July 24—Tuesday</u>

An email to Dr. A

HEY LADY!

This is Kristen Forbes. I'm guessing it might take you a minute to recall who I am. I am the 22 yr old that you got to hang out with at St. Vincent who has cervical cancer and a tumor/mass named Cletus. Remember?! I hope so!

Thank you so much for showing that you cared in the hospital. I have an amazing team of doctors and it's been wonderful!

33

I just want you to know, when I was getting ready for surgery and I was lying there in the OR (Operating Room), I was really nervous and scared, considering it's the first time I was going to be cut open. When you came in, you were singing and dancing and you came up and grabbed my hand and smiled. All my worries immediately went away. I just want you to know that I really appreciate you and your personality! It would not have been as easy for me emotionally to go through that procedure if I didn't have a Dr. like you around! It was great to have you as one of my doctors. Ok well I think I wrote enough for you. Email me back. Hope you are having a wonderful day and are enjoying the place where you are practicing.

Hope to hear from you soon.

Thanks again for everything.

Kristen

*   *   *   *

To my sister Marcia

Sis,

Am I holding up? Every morning I sit up in bed, swing my feet over the edge, sit there in the dark and ask God if I am just having a bad dream. God says to me each morning "NO! Now get to the hospital!"

God tells us that the reason bad things happen to good people is so that the other people are given an opportunity to minister, love and care for them. It is quite apparent too. Without even asking, our next door neighbor mowed our lawn, our church family took up a special collection Sunday morning to fund gas and meals ($369) for all of us, sent us tons of cards, visited us in the hospital, called to encourage us, and most importantly prayed for us. The nurse said today that she has never seen a patient's room look like Kristen's . . . . all the flowers, gifts, and balloons. It has been a humbling experience for our family. Megan and Kristen's friend Chelsea have spent every night with Kristen and given Brenda and me a chance to sleep in our own bed . . . true angels of mercy.

Love,
Kirk

<u>July 26—Thursday</u>

I had my CT scan done today to see the new insides (minus two lymph nodes) and have my "marks" (3 black X's) put on my body to prepare me for my radiation treatment which will start in a week. Once again I had something put in my yoohoo so they could get a better look. Yea!

My cousin from Virginia came to visit today. They gave me beautiful flowers.

* * * *

Just when Kristen was at her lowest mental point, her cousin miraculously shows up with a beautiful flower bouquet. You could see Kristen transition from depressed to lighting up with a wonderful smile and joy in her words.

Eric brought back sand from his summer Florida vacation and put it in Kristen's hospital room. He added a miniature, lighted palm tree so she could brag about having the only hospital room with a private beach.

Kristen was assigned nurse, D. The first time I spoke with her she was very concerned. I could tell she was a seasoned veteran. When I was alone with her, she said "I am so sorry for Kristen to be so young and have this degree of cancer". Suddenly, reality set in for me and I knew Kristen was fighting for her life.

* * * *

Dear Mr. (CEO):

My daughter Kristen Forbes (22) has advanced cervical cancer and was treated at your facility. My wife, Brenda, and I wanted to send you a letter regarding the level of care we received by your associates and employees. What you have to realize is that we have never had a child spend an extended stay in a hospital before, let alone an illness of this magnitude. This is a very stressful time in our lives. Brenda and I, and our entire family want to say thank you many times over. Your personnel who have crossed our paths on this tough journey have been nothing short of miraculous. We have been so impressed with not only the skill, knowledge, and talent of every doctor and nurse but . . . the compassion and love shown by all of them has been both humbling and remarkable.

From the wonderful doctors to the nurses to even the cleaning lady who said she was praying for Kristen and the OR transporter who said God would take good care of our daughter to the caring touch of the OR nurses. We have run out of words to describe how wonderful the quality of care has been. You are truly blessed to have all of these talented and compassionate associates and employees.

Once again . . . many, many thanks. May the Lord continue to bless your medical work.

Sincerely,

Kirk & Brenda Forbes

The Princess has left the building.

July 28—Saturday

"The Princess has left the building!" . . . I told Kristen that whenever an Elvis concert ended his manager would announce "The King (or Elvis) has left the building." That should have been the announcement in the hospital when we took Kristen home yesterday.

She spent a few hours in her apartment to check on her kittens and rest a while. Then big sister went and picked her up and brought her to our house for an overnight. She is moving slow from the surgery but her spirits are up. For the first time in years, all of the family, Mom, Dad, Megan, Eric and Kristen sat and ate supper at the same table. It was wonderful seeing everyone chow down on Mom's fresh mashed potatoes smothered in homemade chicken noodles. Then we sat around, played Disney Trivia with Eric's girlfriend Jamie and watched a movie. Kristen made it through all of it. Kristen melted down and said she was crying because she couldn't say thank you enough to everyone who visited, wrote cards, put her on prayer lists and sent up powerful prayers. So . . . I . . . Dad . . . pass along that thank you.

She has to go to the hospital every day starting Monday for blood draws and give herself daily Lovenox shots for blood thinning. Then sometime next week radiation and chemo begin.

Keep praying.

July 29—Sunday

I tried to lie in bed at night but the pain in my right pelvis feels almost like a cramp and the pain shooting up and down my right leg is almost unbearable! I've had it almost all day today, but I was also up most of the day. I don't know if the two correlate or what because I'm no doctor. ☺ By about 6:30 pm my lower back on the right side started to hurt, so I laid down. Ever since leaving the hospital and going to the pharmacy to get my pain meds, I have been taking two pills every four hours. As I tried to go to bed, my right leg, pelvic area and lower back all hurt. I would rate on a 1-10 scale about a 14. This is the first it has hurt this long and this bad. I don't know if whatever is causing the pain (Cletus the mass) is either getting bigger or worse. I took maybe two extra pain pills because it also seems that the meds are no longer helping. I am now up wide awake because of this pain at 3 am. I am studying the Bible and praying God will help me since these meds obviously will not. Well I'm going to go back to His Word. I thought it would be important that I record the wonderful pain all day and night.

<u>July 30—Monday</u>

Four issues:

Pain . . . Sunday all day and last night. Had to take more than usual. I wake up after 4-5 hours because of pain since the drug wears off. Pain has been getting worse.
Sleep . . . . is there anything I can take to keep me asleep through the night?
Yellowish Leakage . . . . Natural or sign of infection
Bruise on my right hip bone, about the size of a quarter. Don't know where it is from, very sensitive to touch and slightly painful.

Called on-call Doctor. Awaiting a call back because office doesn't open till 9am

the thoughts in my mind
were once so important that
I wrote them all down
I am such a machine now
being hurt too many times
and school
and work
I will never forget this feeling
It will help me be great

—Kristen

Treatments

August 1—Wednesday

Today turned out to be a trial run. We went to radiology for final tattoos for targeting. Then we made a run to the chemo therapy location to get four prescriptions for nausea prevention, nausea treatment, anti-inflammatory, and something else.

Cisplatin is the chemotherapy drug Kristen will be on. Cisplatin is a platinum based compound and is used to treat various cancers. It was discovered in 1845 and FDA approved it in 1978. I told Kristen that platinum is the most expensive metal known to man.

Cisplatin acts by cross linking (damaging) cell DNA in several different ways, making it impossible for rapidly dividing cells to duplicate their DNA for mitosis (process in which a cell duplicates its chromosomes to generate two identical cells). The damaged DNA sets off DNA repair mechanisms, which activate apoptosis (process of deliberate suicide by a cell) when repair proves impossible. Man, medical knowledge and technology are mind blowing.

Tomorrow at 8:45 am is radiation therapy (about 30 mins) then on to chemo for five hours.

Pray for minimal side effects.

Dad

August 2—Thursday

It was a long day today. Kristen had to be at the Radiology Clinic at 8:45 am. They did her target areas with a better "tattoo", and then four blasts of radiation for seven seconds and one for eleven seconds.

Then we went to the Oncology Clinic for Cisplatin chemo. It was about 11 am when they started the series of IV's. She had a bag of magnesium, a bag of potassium, and not sure what else. The nurses were once again wonderful. She finally got unhooked around 4:30 pm.

It is off to radiation again tomorrow. Then Kristen gets Saturday and Sunday off before starting again on Monday.

Thank you for your continued prayers. We know that she is in God's care. He is working through an outstanding group of compassionate doctors and nurses that He has placed in Kristen's path.

August 3—Friday

Today was day two of radiation. She shows no signs of chemo side effects from the Cisplatin. God bless modern medicine. They gave her several drugs to fight nausea and what does she do? Hits Wal-Mart last night and Fryes Electronics today. What a gift. This is one humble Dad saying "Thank you, Lord".

She gets the weekend off then on Monday Week #2 of treatment begins.

* * * *

Dr. D,

Once again . . . many thanks for doing such a great job with Kristen!

Yesterday she completed her first round of chemo and radiation. She is doing extremely well so far. We are hoping and praying for minimal side effects and maximum effectiveness.

I have a couple of questions for you.

Monday is Kristen's two week point since surgery and she is doing very well with it. Everything is healing and no signs of infection. Could she start driving a little? It would make her whole weekend.

Secondly, I was reading that MD Anderson's Medical Center for Cancer is using laparoscopic surgery for this type of cancer. Is there any possibility this technique can be used if she needs further surgery?

Thanks many times.

A very grateful Dad

August 5—Sunday

Yesterday was Kristen's first day off. No pain yesterday so she began weaning herself off of Vicodin. No side effects from treatment yet. The doctor said she could start driving once she got off the Vicodin so . . . she took a short jaunt in her Mustang. She said it felt great. I met her and a girlfriend. We shopped for a desk for her and had lunch out. It was great for Dad to sit across the table and see my smiling daughter laughing and enjoying herself.

Once again . . . many thanks for your prayers and support. You can see God working miracles in her life already. When this journey began Kristen said she knew God had a plan for her. I can see it unfolding before my very eyes.

Dad

August 8—Wednesday

Kristen is down for the count. She developed a cold. Doctors hit her with antibiotics. She is so fatigued she sleeps most of the day. Tough times have begun. I went back to work Monday. Who knows when Kristen might feel up to working.

Megan, who teaches school in Orlando, is going home Saturday because she has teacher prep next week.

Kristen has her second round of chemo tomorrow . . . going to be a long day. Radiation at 10 am and chemo 11am to 4pm.

August 20—Monday

Friday Kristen crossed the halfway point in her treatment. She is still on pain medication but the pain is well controlled. No major nausea problems. She has had four good days in a row. She made it to church with us yesterday. This is the first time in two months. Lots of people came up to her before and after the service and gave her hugs and words of encouragement. During the prayer part of the service our Pastor pointed out that Kristen was there and everyone gave her a round of applause. It really tugged on my heartstrings. We went to her favorite Mexican Buffet for lunch afterward and she ate heartily . . . obviously the treatment has not affected her appetite.

She spent Saturday night with us and before supper she got a call from a pharmacy tech from the Walgreens where she worked. W told her she was diagnosed with cervical cancer too. She had lots of questions and concerns for Kristen to address. After Kristen spent a half hour on the phone with her, she told me that she knows how important it was to be able to help her friend.

We spent Saturday afternoon shopping for high iron food to help fight the anemia. It is amazing finding out what cereals and other foods are high in iron. Kristen thought it was really fun to shop for steaks on sale. Of course, these are high in iron too.

Once again . . . many thanks for your prayers . . . from a grateful Dad.

August 22—Wednesday

Kristen finished her 15th radiation treatment today. She has 10 more to go before she will have the internal radiation. Dr H (Radiology Oncology) explained more about it. She will go into the hospital for 48 hours of treatment. She will be flat on her back. After the internal treatment, she will continue doing the external radiation treatments which will be more intense. Then two weeks later, she will go back into the hospital for the 2nd internal treatment.

Tomorrow is chemo treatment #4. They give her steroids with her chemo. She gets a boost of energy and feels pretty good until it wears off. She is getting sores on her tongue, but a special mouthwash is supposed to help with that side effect. She had a bloody nose yesterday. Kristen felt good enough on Sunday morning to go to church with us. We are all so grateful for the continued prayers for Kristen and our family.

Kristen said that of all the members of our family, she is glad she is the one who has the cancer. It has made her step back and see all of her blessings. She continues to see God at work every day in her life. She recognizes the people that God has placed on her path, the wonderful doctors and nurses, even her kittens. She knows that God placed those kittens in her life so she has someone to greet her in the mornings and keep her laughing.

August 30—Thursday

Kristen finished her 5th treatment of chemo today. Next Thursday will be her last chemo. She will do her radiation treatments Tuesday through Thursday. Then Friday, September 7, she will check into St Vincent's at 5:30 am. She will be put under to place the internal radiation rods next to her uterus. After she wakes up she will go to the Radiation Department for an X-ray and back up to the 6th floor for the weekend. They will check the X-rays and look at how to place the internal radiation pellets (seeds) into the rods. Visitors will be allowed, but only for 30 minutes in a 24 hour period because of the radiation exposure. She will get released sometime on Sunday, after she has 48 hours of the internal treatment. As Dr. H said "You can have your friends lined up down the hallway". I am sure it is going to be a long process for her. I am not sure if they will keep her sedated very much. Something I didn't think about asking. She will be flat on her back the whole time.

She was feeling fairly good today. She drove her car and met me at the medical building. It is only about a five minute drive for her. She has been fighting some nausea and a few other side effects, but the drugs work well. Toward the end of October, Kristen will have a CT scan to see how the treatment has affected the cancer. The chemo and radiation continue to work for four to seven weeks after treatment stops.

Her chemo lasted for four hours today, and in that time she didn't even crack open a coloring book! She looked through magazines the whole time. For those of you who don't know, Kristen has colored since the very beginning, July 13th. It has been about the only thing she has been able to keep focused on.

September 6—Thursday

Sister Megan hung out the whole time ☺

Last chemo! Yea! ☺

Went to Kohl's after Chemo to kill time. Cramping/pain started randomly more on the inside of my right leg . . . horrible pain. Called in Loritab prescription to pick up on way to Dr. H (Radiology Oncologist) appointment.

Meds made pain go away after about 45 minutes.

Dr. H explained procedure and showed us what's going on in my body.

At one point after Dad, Mom and I were waiting for the doctor in the exam room, I noticed how quiet it was and we went to check outside the room. For about 5 minutes we couldn't find anyone. Most of the lights were off and it was past 5pm so we thought everyone left us. Went to the bathroom and just before we left Dr. H walked through the door with two other patients and said he accidentally went to them instead of us first. Ha! Ha! It was just really funny how we all thought that the nurse and doctor forgot about us and left for the day!

Dr. H said he thinks the pain is radiation related. I guess it can affect the tissues and cause pain.

<u>September 7—Friday</u>

Sister Megan is here. ☺ She had flown home for Luke's wedding tomorrow.

Checked in at the hospital about 5:30 am . . . . lots of fun.

Procedure was done around 7 am, the nurse was wonderful. Put my IV in my left arm, best IV ever, and she numbed me before she stabbed me.

Dr. H told my parents while I was in recovery that my cervix and uterus are a little off because the mass (Mr. Cletus) has moved my insides all around.

I was in recovery forever because they couldn't get my pain under control.

Didn't take any of my pain meds and the first nurse when I got up to my room gave me Oxycodone which doesn't do anything and I told her that I need Loritab and my Oxycotin. Took an hour to get and it was horrible. My other nurse, who was an angel, finally got all my pain meds and gave me my Oxycotin, Loritabs and a bigger mg shot of some pain med that starts with a D and it knocked me out.

The X-ray beforehand was a mess because I was in pain. The technician lady noticed and called another to help.

*   *   *   *

Today was fine until Kristen came out of surgery and was in recovery. Her pain meds had worn off. It took until 1:30 pm to get her into her room and get the pain meds she needed. We talked with her radiation doctor. He said that in 2 weeks when this procedure is repeated, they will give her the correct pain medicines. She has a very low pain tolerance and few meds work for her. I hope I said that right, I am beat. She was in pretty bad pain, she "wanted to rip her IV out and go home", "this sucks", "why does it hurt so bad", "I don't want to be here by myself", "no one listens to me about my medicines", etc, etc. The things every parent doesn't want to hear their child say because you can't do anything about it. She had me in tears with how badly she hurt. It wasn't until 6 pm when they got the radioactive seeds in and they will leave them in for 38 hours. Sometimes, even the well trained, best intentioned medical personnel will make mistakes and caregivers have to take an active role. In two weeks we get to go through it all over again.

He did say that he could tell the mass had shrunk.

Mom

September 7—Friday

This internal radiation procedure was very painful. She was alone and had a different staff on a different ward. She had to stay behind portable lead walls surrounding her bed to protect the staff and visitors from high doses of radiation. This treatment causes immediate menopause and kills the ovaries and most of the uterus. Pain, nausea, and constipation but . . . no hair loss . . . she is a real trooper . . . . never complained and has the determination to beat this.

September 9—Sunday

The first internal radiation treatment is over for Kristen. The next one is in two weeks. We brought her home from the hospital at noon today after being flat on her back for the last 38 hours with three rods of radioactive Cesium-137 in her. She had a battle getting the pain in her leg under control Friday evening, but everything else went remarkably well. After they removed the rods she was able to sit up in a chair. Then her Dad walked her around the hallway. Even the nurses were amazed at how well she was doing.

One memorable event during her stay was when Dr. D came to see Kristen. He pulled up a chair and scooted up next to her bed. He patted her arm while he told her how proud he was of her. He said she was an inspiration to everyone and her positive attitude was 95% of her ability to fight this disease. His touch was more of a loving father than a doctor. Sure made this Dad proud too.

Continue the prayers . . . it is very apparent to us all that they are working.

A grateful Dad

<u>September 11—Tuesday 11:26am</u>

Had the internal radiation this past weekend. That sucked and now seems more like a dream. Had to check in Friday at 5am and the procedure was at 7:30am. Guess my cervix and uterus are lying weird because of my mass and now they are going to "boost" the left side with radiation three times. First time was today. So basically I have two more external radiations and one internal left. Done with chemo too. Dr. H said my body should start to recover (bladder and bowels) because of where the treatment is being aimed.

I've been out of work for two months. This is insane.

September 12—Wednesday

Kristen drove and met me at radiation yesterday. They will increase the amount of external radiation to balance the internal radiation. She has today and tomorrow left. Dr. Y gave her a hug goodbye and wished her well.

September 19—Wednesday

Kristen goes into the hospital again on Friday morning to have the internal radiation treatment done again. Dr. H put notes in her file about her pain medicine. If they thought Kristen's Mom and Dad were proactive with pain control last weekend, they haven't seen anything yet. I am picking Kristen up today and taking her to the grocery, blood draw and Michael's Craft store. Tomorrow we go to St V's to see Dr. H.

It looks like she is going to go to Florida with us in October for vacation. We are going to Disney World and we want to get a t-shirt made for Kristen that says "I survived cancer treatment and I'm going to Disney World". She will see Disney World from a wheelchair. It is too much walking for her.

September 21—Friday

Kristen is in the hospital receiving her second internal radiation treatment. The pain is under control this time. Dr. H stayed in recovery with her to make sure the pain meds were controlling the pain. She had the radiation seeds inserted at 5:30 pm and will have them removed at 8:30 Sunday morning. She had some tears today. The catheter makes her bladder hurt, and some pain comes from radiation. Keep those prayers coming.

September 22—Saturday

Kristen is wrapping up her last weekend of internal radiation treatment. We pick her up tomorrow morning at the hospital. It was a rough weekend for her. Her body has become used to the narcotic painkillers. They had to try other meds and chased pain control all weekend. On the brighter side, this is the end of her treatment. She will probably fight side effects for the next week to ten days and then the healing process will begin. We are hoping she will feel well enough to go to Florida with us. Lord knows she really deserves a vacation.

She has been an incredible lady the last three months. She was even able to concentrate enough to read a Harry Potter book. It has been difficult for Kristen to focus on anything because of the drugs. Up to this time she has only been able to color in coloring books.

In 4-6 weeks she will have another CT scan. A future treatment plan will be developed based on the results. We are hoping there will be no need for another round of chemo and radiation. We are praying that the Lord will end this fight tomorrow.

Thank you so much for your visits, prayers, cards and emails, they have sustained all of us through this ordeal.

We will continue to keep you updated on her recovery progress.

A grateful Dad

October 3—Wednesday

I tracked Kristen down last night. She had been out to see a movie and went to Chelsea's for a visit. She has no nausea or pain, but she has been having strong hot and cold flashes. I reminded her that this was the early, radiation induced menopause the doctors had talked about. She is still saying she wants to go to Florida.

*　　*　　*　　*

Ten days have passed since we brought Kristen home from her final radiation treatment. The first few days she chased the nausea problem but kept it in check. The pain seems to be subsiding and the doctors are talking about weaning her off the narcotics. The rest of her internal systems seem to be working better. Kristen is hoping to join us in Florida in a couple of weeks to stick her toes in the hot white sandy beach, visit her sister, Disney World, and relax awhile. She has even talked about going back to work.

Thanks again for your concern and prayers. It is obvious that they have worked in a big way.

A grateful Dad

Sunshine
it's beautiful outside today
stress building
we all look everywhere
for relief
some of them are lucky
enough to find them
find sunshine
I want to see joy
taste happiness
dance around the room
with a SMILE
all over my face

—Kristen

Florida Break—Kristen with the Batch Family

The Break

October 10—Wednesday

Kristen is flying down to Florida on Saturday. Megan lives in Orlando and is picking her up. Kristen has been super fatigued this week. Hopefully, she will not change her mind. I think the beach will do her wonders.

October 13—Saturday

We arrived in Florida on Friday and picked up Kristen at the Orlando airport. She spent the afternoon with us and enjoyed an hour at the beach. You could tell this was a precious moment in her life, as she waded through the waves and soaked up the Florida sun. It was like watching a miracle walking on the beach. She is still wrestling with some pain but is eating better. She will be here in Florida with us until Thursday.

As I drove her to her sister's house in Orlando, we watched the spectacular, red and orange Florida sunset. I could see in her eyes that she had a special appreciation for that moment. This trip is a big step forward and will be full of memories for all of us.

October 22—Monday

She had to take two days to recover from her trip to Disney and SeaWorld. Although exhausted, she really enjoyed the trip. It truly was a blessing to see her smile. Today we took her to St. Vincent's for her PET scan. This will determine if the radiation and chemo treatment was effective, and where we go from here. We meet with the doctor on November 1.

October 22—Monday

Went with Mom and Dad for a CT scan at St. Vincent Hospital. 7:45 am check in time. Had to attempt to drink two huge 16 oz no-ice "crystal light" drinks. It was nasty. Sour cake mix that someone mixed with water as a joke. I was able to drink about ½ of each. After an hour, they took me in for my scan. Wasn't too bad didn't bother me at all. I was starving since I couldn't eat before the procedure so we stopped at Wendy's on the way back to my apartment. I believe I slept on and off for the rest of the day.

<u>October 23—Tuesday</u>

Yesterday morning I had my CT scan to see where everything is at. I just got off the phone with Dr. F's nurse and I guess he said that the results look the same as my other scan? But something looks weird, almost like a shadow. So next Tuesday I have a PET scan scheduled at 7:45 am. I asked the nurse what he meant by "looks the same as the last" because I had a softball size mass so that can't be good. She said she was sorry but all she could say was Dr. F said not to worry. They have also increased my Oxycotin from 20mg to 30mg. I think I might try to go to the Fishers office Thursday to ask Dr. F.

Just kind of scared.

Matt 25: 14-31
Parable of the talents

October 23—Tuesday

I am learning more about cancer treatment. It is like taking two steps forward then one back. Kristen had a CT scan to determine the effectiveness of the treatment . . . that was yesterday. Today the Doctor's office calls and says the scan looked like the first one, "but don't worry, we think it is only a shadow" . . . uh, huh . . . don't worry . . . tell my daughter that. We now have a PET scan scheduled for October 30th. The PET scan should show if the original tumor is still there and the CT scan was faulty. The reason the PET scan was not planned is because of "false positives" created by the radiation induced inflammation.
More prayers are needed.

A very grateful Dad

<u>November 1—Thursday</u>

QUESTIONS FOR THE DOCTOR

Am I able to go to the dentist office?
Only for a cleaning

Why has my pain area changed?
The mass could be moving. The healing process is not easy and will pull and stretch on a few things trying to heal. Pain can also be from having damaged tissue caused by the radiation.

What still causes my leg to swell?
Clot has damaged my veins

How long will I be on blood thinner?
Life long . . . still can obstruct vein and cause another clot

What are the long term effects of surgery and other treatment?

Details about Erbitux Phase 2 trials?

Any patients in the clinical trial?

Have you ever had any patients go to MD Anderson Cancer Center in Houston for further investigative procedures?

Why not just do the same treatment since we know how my body reacted?

Are there other pain drugs or plan that we can use to control "breakthrough" pain?

*   *   *   *

Dr. F (Oncologist) basically had this to say. There is still a mass but they aren't sure if it's cancerous. You can't really be 100% sure of these things because of false readings. He personally looked at the scans so he could see for himself. Said he talked to and sent my test results over to Dr. D (Gyn-Oncology Surgeon). He is going to decide if he wants to perform surgery on me or if there is a better plan for action. Hopefully, I'll be meeting with him either Mon, Tues or Wed.

Thursday I have another Dr. F appointment where we will discuss other options for treatment if I am not going to have surgery. There is a clinical trial for a cancer drug, and they may try it on me to see if it works. The clinical trial is being performed here in Indy. We didn't really go into it because it's not important yet.

My pain has shifted to the outside of my thigh and hip. It feels like I've slept on that leg for 2 weeks straight and then the pain is down my whole leg. He increased my Oxy to 40 mg.

I had to step out of the exam room to throw up. As soon as I left, he shut the doors, looked at my parents and asked them how they were. Later on he said very thoughtful words about how wonderful it is to get compliments from patients and that some will go as far as to write to the CEO of the hospital (Dad's letter). Then he said he couldn't talk about it without having tears come to his eyes.

That's what an awesome doctor I have!

*　　*　　*　　*

On Tuesday Kristen had a PET scan done because last week's CT scan was inconclusive. Based on the PET scan, Dr. F told us that the cancer activity in the pelvic tumor (size of a softball) has been reduced by 60%. He said the next step is to discuss these results with Dr. D, Kristen's original surgeon. Dr. D operated back in July and decided not to attempt to remove the mass because it was involved with a major vein, artery, nerve and muscle. He said if it was his daughter he would do the radiation/chemo and then take a second look. Now we wait to hear from Dr. D to see if he would do a second surgery given the results so far. If he says no then Dr. F wants to try to get Kristen into a clinical trial using the drug Erbitux that is currently used in patients with advanced colon or head and neck cancer which have the same type of cancer cell structure as cervical cancer.

Was this the news we wanted? Honestly . . . no . . . I was hoping the radiation and chemo had worked better.

Need prayers more than ever now.

A grateful Dad

November 4—Sunday

I believe I do the same . . . . nothing . . . almost every single day.

I fall into the same pattern everyday
unsure if I am keeping up with the
world around
all things pass by
but is it starting to fade too quickly

—Kristen

<u>November 7—Wednesday</u>

Went and talked to Dr. D (Gyn-Oncology Surgeon) about surgery today. Found out in the waiting room that I would be having an exam. Yea, but it went well and actually wasn't too awkward with Dr. D. Afterwards he, the nurse, Mom, Dad and I we got started. Total time of the meeting with him was about 1hr 30mins. Most of it was chit chatting. Well, he said that he did not want to perform surgery on me but rather have a PET scan again at the end of November or beginning of December so they can get a better reading. He gave us a copy of both of my PET scans and answered questions I had about the language. He drew pictures that really helped. The surgery that he would have performed would be very serious and extensive. He would be removing my female parts, my bladder, part of my gall bladder and some of the leg muscle that my mass is sitting on. It was funny because Dr. D recalled that I named the mass. Everyone was trying to recall the name when all of a sudden he goes "Oh, yeah, it's Cletus!" ha, ha, ha! I just think he is an amazing doctor. I can show him my vacation pictures; he remembers what I name my mass. Before I left, my Dad tried to brag about how he got a hug from Dr. D so I turned around and got one too. He thanked Dad for the letter he wrote to the CEO. When he was talking about it, you could tell he was fighting back tears. Dr. D looked me straight in the eye and told me what a wonderful patient I was and that I was a good person blah, blah, blah. So that was awesome as well. He told us he would call Dr. H and give him an update for us. After I get my PET scan scheduled I am going to set up an appointment with Dr D.

<u>November 8—Thursday</u>

Dr. F (Oncologist) showed up 40 mins late so I am taking the time to catch up on my medical journal. Today we are going to discuss the different options of treatment. I am going to ask what my options for pain meds are because the 40mg twice a day are not working. And for some reason my last refill for the Hydros they gave me were 7.5/750mg instead of 500mg. My nurse friend said there is no particular reason they can't give me the 750 and that I should ask. I can't take more than five of these pills in 24 hours because of the Tylenol. After these five pills there are still a few times during the day when I am in pain. I can't do anything because I've taken all the pills that I can. I don't know if he will increase my Oxy dosage. I talked to Dr. D about it and he said there is a possibility that I have a tolerance to them or something. It's now 10:08 am and my appt was at 9:15 am. At least I'm not here for chemo . . . at least not yet.

November 9—Friday

Two days ago we met with Kristen's Oncology Surgeon Dr D. As of now, surgery is not an option. It would involve too much, and be a major, life changing surgery for Kristen. Dr D would like Kristen to have another PET scan done on December 20th, and then see her again. They get too many false readings this soon after treatment because inflammation caused by radiation can look like cancer. The body is still metabolizing the treatments and in four to six weeks they would get a better picture.

Yesterday was a meeting with Dr. F and we discussed treatment options. Last week he talked about chemotherapy and a clinical trial drug Erbitux for cervical cancer. Erbitux is currently in Phase II trials for cervical cancer.

Dr. D told Kristen how much he enjoys working with her and her family. She brings out the best in him and she is an inspiration to him. She has decisions to make and a lot to think about on what the next course will be. She celebrates her 23rd birthday next Thursday November 15th.

Thanks for all your prayers for Kristen.

A grateful Dad

November 24—Saturday

Kristen has an appointment with her Oncologist on December 7th. It is a routine monthly checkup and probably more discussion about getting into the clinical trial for Erbitux. Kristen has already decided that she wants to try it, if she can get into it. They are only accepting 4 women in Indiana and 19 nationwide for this trial. She has a PET scan scheduled for December 20th. I assume she would start the trial after the holidays, if she is accepted.

Right now they are still trying to get the pain under control. She has been on two different narcotics plus a supplement. The supplement is being changed to find the right drug to control the pain, so she can return to work since she has been out since July 13th. They are on the 3rd drug for the supplement. It is Celebrex used for patients with arthritis. The prayer needed now is they find the right supplement so she can return to some semblance of a normal life. Other than the pain, she is doing better.

Thank you again for you support.

A grateful Dad

November 29—Thursday

They put Kristen on Celebrex, the pain med for people with arthritis. She has felt a lot better the last two days. Her pain level is at zero and no nausea or vomiting. She is scheduled to see Dr. F on the 6th and then another PET scan on the 20th. The plan is for sister Megan to fly here for Christmas and then we will drive back to Florida after the 25th. Kristen will fly down to join us.

We don't think they will start Kristen on the clinical trial until after the holidays. So off we go to Florida again.

If you were born a second chance
would you live so you wouldn't fall short of
God's only glory or God's own eyes
would you change yourself
be any different from now
is this place really worth all the pain it
brings on

—Kristen

Pain Control

December 4—Tuesday

We decided it was time to get a pain specialist involved with Kristen. Pain is now a specialty all in itself. I was told many years ago by a doctor that in this day and age NOBODY needs to suffer with chronic pain. One way or another it can be controlled. He told me that if someone you know is suffering from chronic pain you need to be proactive. He said to locate the largest Medical Center nearby and call the head of the Anesthesiology Department. If he can not help you, he will definitely be able to refer you to a pain specialist who can. So I got online and found the head of the Anesthesiology Department at our local Medical Center. I sent him an "I need your help" email briefly explaining Kristen's medical history. Within two hours I had an email back from him listing four doctors at the IU Medical Center that specialize in cancer pain. Wow . . . . was I impressed! Two days later I received a phone call from a nurse saying they will work Kristen in immediately . . . . When can you get her in? I am impressed again.

*   *   *   *

1. Pain specialist . . . a must.

2. Would physical therapy help . . . considering where the damage is?

3. I read in an MD Anderson Cancer Newsletter that the PET scan is now being used as a weapon against cancer. It doesn't damage the good cells so there is little or no collateral damage and no major side effects. Could this be something that would be beneficial to Kristen?

4. Is Kristen definitely in the clinical trial for Erbitux? If so can she go to Florida before starting the trial?

<u>December 6—Thursday</u>

QUESTIONS FOR THE DOCTOR

I still have pain throughout the day. Is there something else I can take . . . or a pain specialist that I can see?

What's my status regarding the clinical trial?

Once I schedule a cleaning with my dentist should I skip my Coumadin the day before?

Physical Therapy?

Florida first two weeks of January?

Can HPV be detected through any blood test? Any way at all to test males?

December 8—Saturday

Kristen saw Dr. F yesterday. They are still trying to get the pelvic pain under control. We stepped in and said "time to see a Pain Specialist". So we are working on that right now. Hopefully, next week she can see one. Everyone asks what is causing the pain. It could be several possibilities; the cancer, the radiation side effects or the damage the cancer or radiation has caused to the bone, muscle or nerves in that area. There are many ways to block the pain signal. They can use the narcotics she is already on, complete nerve blocks and several methods in between.

She is still scheduled for a PET scan. Dr. D told her that he now uses her analogy to explain the scan to new patients. Kristen told him cancer has a sweet tooth and the IV sugar is absorbed by the cancer and reflected in the PET scan images. The scan is on December 20th, followed by a meeting with Dr. F the next day to review the results. I am still praying that God will work a grand miracle and the scan will be clear.

Again . . . thanks for all the prayers.

A grateful Dad

December 11—Tuesday

Kristen has been referred by her doctor to Pain Specialist Dr. P at St. V's.

December 12—Wednesday

Email to Dr. D

Dr. D,

Once again many, many thanks for all your help. I know Kristen and our entire family recognize what wonderful personal care you and the rest of the medical staff have been giving us. Kristen has an appointment to see Dr. F on Thursday.

One more question . . . I was reading a newsletter I get from MD Anderson Cancer Center about how they are using the PET scan as a weapon to fight cancer and not just as an imaging tool. Something about using protons instead of X-rays which do not damage the good cells. Have you heard about this at all?

Thanks again,

Kirk

December 19—Wednesday

Kristen had an appointment last Wednesday with Dr. P, the cancer pain doctor. The pain she is experiencing is from the radiation. He also increased her Celebrex.

Kristen still suffers from bouts of nausea. Some days she rates her pain as a 1 or 2 other days as a 3 or 4. She spends most of the day lying on the sofa. It is the most comfortable position for her and keeps the pressure off the area causing her pain.

December 21—Friday

Yesterday was Kristen's PET scan and today we met with Dr. F. He said he was not happy with the results. The scan indicates no spreading of the cancer to other organs but there is new activity around the outside perimeter of the original tumor. This can be new cancer or it can be inflammation from the radiation treatment. The doctors have to assume it is new cancer activity and treat it as such. Dr. F has talked with Dr. E who is heading up the clinical trial for Erbitux chemotherapy. We have a meeting with Dr. E Dec. 27th to discuss getting Kristen into the clinical trial. There is stress on the ureter tube that runs from her right kidney to the bladder which could cause the tube to close. He wants her to see a Urologist to determine if they should put a stent in this tube to protect her kidney.

The new pain medications (Neurotin and Celebrex) seem to be helping with the pain, but it is still an issue. Kristen has a follow-up with the pain doctor on December 26th.

<u>December 25—Tuesday—Christmas Day</u>

First and most important . . . MERRY CHRISTMAS . . . to all who read my words. I was sitting here in my hotel room thinking about all the children in the community and city around me . . . getting up excitedly, running in and waking their parents and roaring into the family room to start digging into the pile of Christmas presents. I hope they are equally excited about the true meaning for the season.

It is easy to feel a little bummed when you are away from home and working on Christmas but then I think about all the other dedicated professionals doing the same thing; the police, fire fighters, medical personnel, airline, rail and truck employees. Suddenly I realize I am not alone, even though the hotel customer service person, Pat, told us we were the only two guests in the hotel last night.

The Forbes family celebrated Christmas last Friday night when Megan airlined in from Orlando and got home about 11 pm. At first we decided to open just one present. Then it grew to <u>all</u> the presents, and finally Dad had to call a halt to the celebration at 2 am because "I have to go to work in a few hours." We laughed a lot and had a wonderful time . . . first time in four years that the whole family gathered together for a Christmas. Even though the last 6 months have been consumed by Kristen's battle against cancer, we were able to pause and savor the moment of Christmas. We couldn't have done it without all the prayer support, phone calls, cards, visits and wonderful acts of kindness shown to us this year.

I wanted to say thank you to all of you and wish you the most wonderful Christmas and 2008 that God has planned for you.

Merry Christmas . . . from my hotel room.

Kirk

PS . . . Attached is our Christmas photo for this year . . . from left to right . . . Megan (27), Kristen (23), Jamie (Eric's girlfriend) and Eric (21)

Megan, Kristen, Jamie and Eric Christmas Photo

December 28—Friday

Yesterday Kristen had an appointment with Dr E, the doctor heading up the clinical trial for Erbitux. At this time, Kristen doesn't meet the criteria for the clinical trial. The treatment that Kristen has already had, radiation with Cisplatin chemotherapy, doesn't qualify her. She needs an additional full chemotherapy treatment to be looked at as a candidate. So now we wait for Dr. F to set up the next chemotherapy program.

Kristen had an appointment with Dr. P for pain on Wednesday. Since the Neurotin didn't completely eliminate the pain, he switched her to a new drug, Lyrica. She started on that today and should be able to tell in four days if it works.

She has an appointment with Dr N, a Urologist, on January 9th, to see if she needs a stent put in her ureter. The PET scan showed some blockage which they feel is from the radiation treatment.

Kristen had tears today, felt she wasted her time having the meeting with Dr. E about the clinical trial, tired of not being able to do anything but lie on her sofa and deal with pain.

January 1—Tuesday

Florida for Christmas break. This was not a good trip to Florida for Kristen. She was trying to get used to a new pain medication and the side effects of the radiation. Fatigue was a huge issue. Kristen spent 90% of her time in bed.

<u>January 8—Monday 6 am</u>

Back home in my apartment after Florida trip

It almost seems that every night my "falling asleep" problem is becoming worse. The couch is almost my new bed because it is much more comfortable when I am in pain. My pain is probably 3-4; I took Ibuprofen so it should start to feel better soon. I took two Ambien around 3 am and obviously no effect because I am still up and now writing about it. The problem really seems to be all the meds I am on, I just don't get tired. It sucks. It's so hard on your heart. I'm already having problems with my pulse rate and blood pressure. So yea, for all of that because my body isn't busy enough dealing with chemo and all the aftermath of radiation. At least I'm strong enough not to go crazy with all of this . . . or at least not yet.

Awesome! Just checked the clock and guess what time it is? No really guess. Oooooohhhh so close. It is now 7:00 am. I almost feel like I should pull an all nighter and then go to bed real early. Not like I do anything all day but lay here.

Well, I could take another Ambien but that would be the 3rd and I'd be asleep until 7 pm.

Both those options are bad. I think I'll just lay here and watch the History Channel and hope it bores me to sleep. I need a kitty to snuggle with. Great, I'm now starting to get really bad dry mouth. And the Ibuprofen hasn't started to work. In truth, I think the pain is getting worse. Ok, I'm going to grab something liquid to satisfy my dry mouth and snuggle on the couch.

Sweet! I just found my journal. Saved by the bell, so maybe this whole thing will pan out. Wish me luck and hopefully I'll keep this journal and you'll know how it turns out.

Goodnight or should I say Good Morning . . . . Kristen

PS . . . . here comes the sun!

*   *   *   *

<u>1:45pm</u>

Yea, so I never fell asleep and surprisingly I'm still going at it. It has to be all the meds I'm on or something, I don't know. Chelsea and I are going to hang out this afternoon. I'm excited because I need my Chelsea fix bad. I miss her a lot. I am just so glad that I have her as one of my best friends. She is so amazing. What she does and just the person that she is.

Upstairs neighbor is playing music really loud again. It's 2 pm on a Monday? I don't know why either is home. Their music system must be DIRECTLY above my couch, which sucks because well 1—it's loud and 2—I can't turn up the TV loud enough to cover it up. At least for the moment its good music and not the crazy rap like usual . . . . knock on wood.

I use to write all the time, I have tons of journals. To be honest, it feels really good to write again.

I need to get back into writing poems. I'm good at it and it is a wonderful outlet.

Ok, I need to start on it and get in the shower before Chelsea shows up.

Kristen

<u>January 16—Wednesday</u>

Meeting with Dr. N (Urologist)

Right Kidney pretty well shutdown
Place a stent and change every 3-4 months
Community North Surgery Center with anesthesia

<u>January 17—Thursday</u>

Meeting with Dr. F

Talked about chemo and he asked when I was ready to start treatments. I told him the truth, ASAP! He said alright then and proceeded to put his hand on my back and kind of push me and told me to go find a chemo chair.

With this chemo I'll have it for 2 weeks then off 3rd week then on for 2 weeks and then off and I'll have a scan. This chemo only takes about 2 hours instead of the 5-6 hours of the last type.

<u>January 21—Monday</u>

Today is the day I'm to get a stent between my kidney and bladder. Lately it feels like my pain has changed and it could be this or my new medicine. Who knows? I just feel like I have to pee really badly and then when I try there is nothing. Maybe it is because of the pressure from my mass/tumor. Either way I hope Dr. N gets it right the first time and everything is all better. I guess they have to change the stent every 3-4 months.

Yea!

Hope this goes well.

*   *   *   *

Today was stent placement in the ureter tube between the right kidney and bladder. Dr N told us about the procedure and said, the anesthesiologist, Dr. S would be in shortly. Small world . . . and a miracle . . . Dr. S was Kristen's grandparents' neighbor and one of their best friends. Her grandparents passed away many years ago but because of this connection Kristen said "Grandpa and Grandma are telling me it is going to be fine today."

The stent procedure took 20 minutes and an hour in recovery. She had her sense of humor and entertained us with her wit. As she drifted in and out of sleep, she helped Eric with his finance homework.

We brought her home with us for a few hours to recover from the anesthesia. Then I saw another miracle happen. Kristen has not been able to sit upright since September without pain in her pelvis. Normally she would have headed straight for the couch to keep pressure off that area. Instead she went right to the computer. She got online, paid some bills and checked her email. She never went for the couch. I realize to most people this would be insignificant, but she has not been able to do this in four months.

Thanks for the prayers. It was a reminder today with Dr. S that God is still in control. She goes in on Thursday for her second treatment of chemotherapy. Last week was pretty hard on her during the treatment. Please pray for a more comfortable therapy.

Thank you so much for keeping hope alive for Kristen.

A very humble but elated Dad

PS . . . let us celebrate the small victories!

*   *   *   *

For those of you who have not fought the cancer fight with a loved one, let me try to tell you how exhausting it is both emotionally and physically.

On Monday Kristen had a blood draw which found her hemoglobin had dropped into the danger range (7.0), so a blood transfusion was ordered to add red blood cells. This required going to the hospital on Friday.

On Tuesday Kristen had an appointment with her pain doctor. He wants to try another pain drug, Cymbalta, in conjunction with Lyrica, which will hopefully ease the pain she still experiences each day. This will be in addition to the two narcotics she is on already for baseline and breakthrough pain control.

Wednesday, she met with her Urologist. She had her stent put in today. They will put her under for the procedure.

Thursday was her oncologist who gave Kristen her first round of chemo (a cocktail of two chemo drugs).

She cried again today. She is very tired of being sick and not feeling up to doing anything. She did go to Florida over Christmas but spent most of her time sleeping in the hotel. Megan, Kristen and Dad spent about 3 hours at the Animal Kingdom, spent one afternoon at Universal Park and got her to the beach one day.

She sleeps a lot, and we aren't sure now if it is a side effect of the pain medication or because she is anemia. She has a hard time sleeping at night, so hopefully this new medicine will help ease the pain.

We spent today at the hospital for a blood transfusion which lasted from 8 am till 4 pm. Kristen did well. She never complained about the pain.

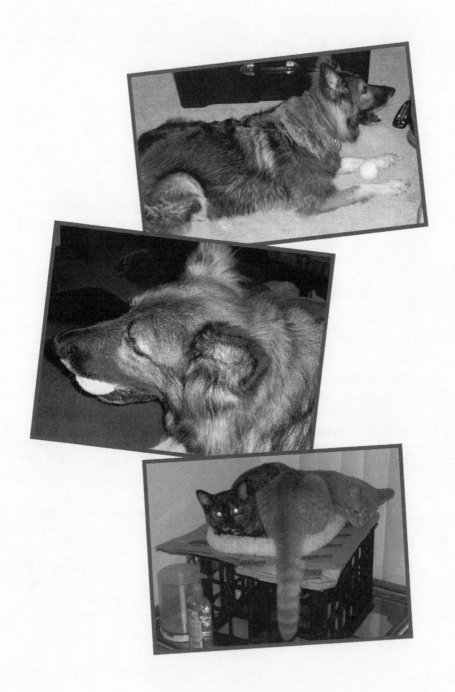

Duchesse, Fiji and OJ

<u>January 31</u>

10:50 pm

Let me give you the scene of my apartment, this will be fun to look back on someday.

It's probably 20-30 degrees F outside and we have been under a winter storm warning. I am watching Celebrity Rehab on VH 1.

3:47 am

Fiji is cracked and I mean CRACKED out, scattering everywhere. Kind of funny to watch. I am sitting at the kitchen table getting some things done and I have Juice (OJ) in sight licking himself like crazy and when he starts to walk around he is shaking each foot, really hilarious. Why you ask? Well, the kitties are allowed to walk, climb, play, everywhere but my desk and kitchen counter. For some reason, Juice has started (about a month ago) to jump up on the kitchen counter. Basically, no discipline works.

So a few days ago he jumped on the counter DIRECTLY in front of me. That was a mistake. I grabbed the stinker, marched into the bathroom, turned the faucet on a comfortable temp and stuck him under it and got his shoulders to his tail SOAKED. And guess what, no more jumping on the counter. Aaha! Now he doesn't even think about doing it anymore. Yea! I was pleased with the results. ☺

Yea, so there is your picture of what's going on. I slept four to five hours. Last night, I took my pills later than usual, on top of the fact that I'm already super exhausted.

* I FEEL TIRED *

<u>February 5—Tuesday</u>

<u>12:00 am</u>

We had to go to Dr. F's office on 86th street to pick up my Oxy script, dropped off at pharmacy and went to eat at the Café. It's a small café and this really cool lady runs it. It was definitely an experience. Then we headed to St. V's so I could have my blood drawn. Almost back home, my friend mentions going to Target and I say "Let's Go." I need parmesan cheese too. Well about an hour and $200 later we headed back to my place. I decided to splurge and buy the Kitties a jungle gym that on either side has a mouse hanging off the edge. After we had it all set up, they both immediately started to go after the mice. About an hour later they were both lying around and could barely keep their eyes open. All I can say is that I have some good pictures ☺ I'm so thankful that God placed my Kitties in my life. It was really good timing, but then again, God does that.

<u>February 10—Sunday</u>

<u>2:56 am</u>

I didn't have Chemo Thursday because I had a temperature of 102.8 F.

Everyone has left me
no more ears to hear me
now that you have stripped me
take the one thing
you haven't touched
my breath

—Kristen

Setback

February 12—Tuesday

We are on our way to take Kristen to the emergency room at St V's. She has had a swollen right leg for the last week. Today she can't bend the knee because it is so swollen. Dr F wants her to go to the emergency room. We would appreciate all your prayers while the doctors try to find the cause of the swelling. You might remember the swelling is how they found the tumor to begin with. She is on Coumadin, so hopefully it is not a blood clot. We will keep you posted. Thanks for the prayers.

February 13—Wednesday

We had to bring Kristen to the emergency room yesterday. Her leg was badly swollen, running a fever and pain to the point she couldn't walk or move her right leg.

The ER doctor ran an MRI and put her on Dilaudid which is eight times stronger than morphine. She has a high resistance to pain meds. The MRI was inconclusive so they admitted her.

*   *   *   *

Kristen was in the emergency room until 11 pm. She received a chest X-ray and an MRI. The doctor thought she had an abscess that had caused the swelling and temperature. He couldn't tell with the MRI, so they may do surgery.

Her best friend Chelsea is spending the night with her. Kirk and I came home to get some sleep before we head back in the morning in time for doctor rounds. Thank you all for your prayers. When we pulled up in front of the emergency room, there came Meghan with the wheelchair. Meghan is a friend from high school and church and works in the ER.

*   *   *   *

Dr. D told us Kristen's colon is leaking internally and causing infection. This calls for a colostomy. During this surgery, they will look for an abscess that may need to be drained. Will this remedy the leg swelling and pain? No one is sure. The ER surgeon told us last night that the tumor mass was creating problems and should be debulked but Dr. D said that is not an option at this time. It would require "life altering" surgery.

Thanks for all the prayers . . . they have sustained us.

A grateful and exhausted Dad

February 14—Thursday

The bowel surgeon told Kristen how critical it is to stop the infection caused by the leak in the colon. He explained all the options but pointed out the only viable one was a colostomy. He asked Kristen if she would accept the surgery and she said no. To say I was crushed is an understatement. We are talking about survival here and Kristen said no. The surgeon reviewed all the imaging and spoke to all the other doctors to see what options might be available. There were none. I asked Kristen to at least think about it.

Later, I called Dr. D and asked if he would come by and speak to Kristen. I know we can't force her to do anything. It is her body and her life. We will support her in whatever decision she makes. We knew Kristen had high regard for Dr. D's opinion. She might consider his opinion as a second opinion. Dr. D came in this afternoon and talked with her. He told her that thousands of people have colostomies and that is what he would like her to do. She said she wanted to think about it overnight.

Dr. A stopped by and saw Kristen. She is the doctor that came in the operating room, turned up the music, and started dancing. It was a memory that put peace in Kristen's life at that moment.

Kristen's white cell count has dropped from 44,000 to 31,000 this morning. Before they do surgery it needs to get down in the 10,000 area.

February 15—Friday

6:40 am

Dr. F . . . asked about the surgery. Another doctor is on call this weekend. Dr. F will be at a conference this weekend.

* * * *

Kristen said she was ready to get something done. She was tired of not feeling good. She was having lots of pain getting out of bed, moving her leg and using the commode.

Dr D came back this morning and went over the colostomy again with her. Kirk went over it with her too. Dr. T, the bowel surgeon came in and asked her if she had made a decision. She told him she wanted to do it. The surgeon explained the procedure. They would see if they could drain any of the fluid in the pelvic area.

Mom

February 16—Saturday

Kirk and I went home to make lasagna for Kristen for dinner while Eric, Jamie and Megan kept Kristen company. She was hungry for lasagna the other day, and we had bought everything to make it before she went into the hospital. At midnight on Sunday they will cut off her food and liquids in preparation for surgery.

She enjoyed the lasagna. We gave the rest to the nurses. The next day the nurses asked for the recipe.

We are so grateful for the physicians and the nurses that are involved in Kristen's care. It is obvious to us that God has placed each one of them in our path. Dr D stopped by the lounge tonight after 6 pm. He had made the trip all the way from the Oncology Building just to sit and talk with us.

February 17—Sunday

One of the doctors in Dr F's practice was in this morning. She wanted to have an ultra sound done on Kristen's left leg to rule out blood clots. She started her on Lasix, a drug that draws off excess fluids.

Kristen also received an IV of magnesium and a large glass of the potassium. Megan spent last night with her. Kristen didn't do very well. She had pain and didn't want them to draw blood at 4 am. Her best friend Chelsea, whom we consider an angel, is once again spending the night with Kristen.

As of right now, the colostomy surgery is scheduled tomorrow. They may put a PICC line (6) in to allow them to draw blood without sticking Kristen.

February 18—Monday

When Kirk and I were driving to the hospital early this morning, we felt at peace. We knew that we had many people all over the world praying for Kristen. Plus we had a surgeon and nurses that the Great Physician had surrounded us with.

Kristen went to the cardiac lab this morning to have a PICC line put in. One of the great things about a PICC line is they can give IV fluids and draw blood from it.

Kristen's surgery took about an hour and twenty minutes. We went into a conference room to wait for Dr T. He said he wasn't able to drain any of the fluid. He is not sure what is causing the swelling. There was leakage from the colon into the dead tumor. They will continue to give her the antibiotics to stop the infection. Her abdomen is pretty sore from the incision. I haven't looked at it, but the nurse told Kristen it is about 8 inches long.

Dr D stopped by to see how Kristen did with the surgery. Kirk asked him to look at her charts and give us his opinion. He feels that by stopping the source of infection the swelling will go down. Then we can get her back into chemo. Kristen was awake enough to tell Dr D "surgery sucks".

Hopefully the surgery has removed the source of the infection. We hope the high-powered antibiotic continues to fight the infection which has caused her abdomen, legs and feet to swell. They will not release her from the hospital until the infection and pain are under control.

February 19—Tuesday

Kristen had a pretty good day today. She has slept most of it. Her legs are still swollen, but the right leg doesn't hurt as much. She can take nothing by mouth except ice chips. They finally let her have small sips of water. Dr T was in this morning and told her, the more she got up and moved around, the better she would feel.

The Ostomy nurse came in and changed her colostomy bag. Kristen didn't watch and I think it was a reality check for her. Please continue to pray for her adjusting to the colostomy and the stoma to heal. This usually takes six weeks.

We talked to Dr. F this evening. He said she is recovering remarkably well. She has nurse D tonight. He is a good nurse and always makes sure that Kristen is comfortable and has everything she needs.

*   *   *   *

The doctors and nurses have been magnificent with Kristen. Last night Kristen's oncologist remarked that the nurses were very "protective" of Kristen. I can not say enough positive things or give enough thanks to the medical personnel. Even the emergency room doctor and nurse were asking how she was doing and expressed deep concern about her. This is several days after they cared for her in ER.

Very humbling.

Left so unsatisfied
will you ever smile again
your eyes look in mine
empty answers fall behind

—Kristen

The Cancer Rollercoaster

February 21—Thursday

Welcome to the Cancer Rollercoaster. Yesterday afternoon Kristen was doing fine . . . pain under control, antibiotic working on infection, she made it through the colostomy surgery with flying colors and the doctors were telling us to think about taking her home if the trend continues.

Then Kristen had two major seizures. By the time we got from the lounge to her room the Rapid Response team had been summoned (paddles and all); a Neurology doctor and five nurses were also headed for her room. By the time we got to her room, the senior nurse R, was standing near Kristen's head leaning over saying "Kristen, stay with us . . . . Kristen . . . Kristen, stay with us".

Ever have your chest tighten up and your stomach leaps up to just under your chin? . . . yep rollercoaster. I thought for sure we were going to lose her. She was crying and desperately trying to get her IV out and get out of the bed. She had the look of fear and confusion because she didn't know what was happening and didn't recognize us.

They got her stabilized and rushed her down to ICU. They did a CT scan and an MRI to rule out bleeding, infection or tumor in her brain. We spent the night. She slept peacefully. Brenda and I fed her ice chips this morning. She drifted in and out . . . asked where she was. She does not remember the experience. Thank you, God.

Just got a call from Dr. F, her oncologist . . . the CT scan and MRI showed no damage to her brain. They think the seizures may have been triggered by the antibiotic. They will give her anti-seizure medication to stabilize her and hopefully return her to the Oncology floor soon.

I think Brenda and I have re-defined the term mental, physical and emotional exhaustion. Your prayers sustain us . . . nothing else can.

A grateful Dad

*   *   *   *

They temporarily took her off all of her meds to try to isolate the problem. She is on no narcotic pain meds right now and her legs were starting to hurt so we propped them up on pillows. Her white cell count went up again; from 16,000 to 22,000.

Sister Megan is flying back to Florida this morning. Kirk is running her to the airport.

Kristen's sense of humor has survived. She told me to get her Dad from the lounge. She said she would go herself, but she was on bed rest.

*　　*　　*　　*

The MRI showed something that indicated the seizures were caused by the antibiotic she had been on since last Tuesday. They have now changed to a different antibiotic and put her on two anti-seizure drugs.

She had an EEG (brain wave analysis) this afternoon. I think the massaging made her head feel good so she asked us to wash her hair. They are going to move her back up to the 6th floor Oncology wing today.

February 22—Friday

Relief . . . at least for today. Kristen did well. She was awake this morning and ate some breakfast. She spent most of the day sleeping. She is on two anti-seizure medications to prevent future seizures. The pain doctor said they are going to wean her off the Dilaudid and increase the Oxycotin. Her white count continues to go down, indicating the new antibiotics are working. The doctors think that the original antibiotic is what triggered the seizures. Her legs are still badly swollen.

Her sense of humor is back . . . thank you for small miracles. Before she was released from Neuro ICU the neuro doctor asked Kristen several questions to see how her mind was working, not expecting her sense of humor to surface. He asked her:

Do you know what day it is?
"No"

Do you know where you are at?
"Yep . . . in a big facility".

Do you know your name?
"Yes"

Will you tell me what your name is?

"NO".

Do you know my name?
"You should know . . . you've got your name tag on."

Love this kid.

*   *   *   *

She still has a way to go before she gets to checkout. She has not experienced much pain today. Kristen has an "I can do it" attitude, even though she falls asleep halfway through working on something. Last night, we talked with Dr. D about all the instances where God has been involved in Kristen's life. He told us that many doctors and nurses are praying for Kristen and that her "I can do it" attitude has been an inspiration to the staff.

February 23—Saturday

This was a tough day for Kristen. Last night she "slept like crap". Because she ate a little food yesterday her GI tract tried to work and didn't, fought against itself and on came the nausea, the anti-acid and anti-nausea drugs. Between that and the anti-seizure meds she slept all day long. During the brief moments of being awake she was grumpy and depressed over being sick all the time.

On the good side, the lower GI is starting to work. The physical therapist came in and showed her the exercises for her legs to help prevent bed sores and blood clots. He pulled her up to an almost sitting position and that caused some pain. Other than that, her pain has been under control.

I have been astounded at how Kristen has affected so many people she has met. It is almost profound. When the physical therapist finished his session he walked to the end of the bed and stood there quietly watching her drift off to sleep. You could see in his eyes for that brief moment he was really touched by this solitary life. The compassion was amazing. He very thoughtfully said, "Kristen, you are going to make it . . . you are going to be ok." I almost lost it . . . for a moment in time everything stopped and we were both affected by this young lady.

Thanks for the support, balloons, cards (many from all over the country) and prayers,

A very, very grateful Dad

February 24—Sunday

Senior nurse R, who was telling Kristen to "stay with us" during her seizures, is a shining star. He became very attached to Kristen and our family. One day he came in and gave Kristen two of his own stuffed animals. She happily accepted his gifts . . . ."El Torro the Love Bull" and "I love Chocolate" the Bear. Both sing and speak when you squeeze their feet. This was just another touch of compassion by the wonderful staff.

February 26—Tuesday

Kristen got out of bed and hobbled to a chair. That is the first time since she had a seizure on Wednesday afternoon. It wore her out, but you could tell she was pleased with herself.

Dr. F was in to see Kristen this morning before I got in. Best friend Chelsea spent the night with her. The doctor said she may go home on Thursday. She has to be able to get up and walk before that happens. Dr I, the infectious disease doctor, has changed her IV antibiotics to pill form, so she can go home. Her Oxycodone is back up to the level she was on before she came into the hospital two weeks ago. The neurologist was in and reduced the dosage of one of the anti-seizure drugs today.

Kristen stayed awake with her friends Chelsea and Jeff last night for a couple of hours. This is a hard thing for her to do while on pain meds and anti-seizure drugs. Her case worker came by and talked with Kristen about home visiting nurses. The case worker is from our town . . . small world.

Mom

* * * *

Dr. F is talking about Kristen going home tomorrow. At least the way things are progressing, it will be this week. She has told the case manager that she is going home to stay a while with her parents.

The nurse had Kristen in a chair yesterday and she was able to sit for about 15 minutes. Her knees were a little wobbly getting back into bed. The physical therapist was in this morning and had her sit in a chair. The Ostomy nurse was in this morning so we could learn more about her appliance.

The one piece of exciting news is that when I got here this morning she was "starving". I had brought her some yogurt, and she ate about half of it. It was good to see her appetite coming back.

Kristen is slowly making her way through her stack of cards. Her anti-seizure drugs make her pretty sleepy, but she is staying awake longer. Chelsea said they stayed up and talked until about 11:30 last night.

<u>February 28—Thursday</u>

The doctors are sending Kristen home today. Because her hemoglobin is low, they are giving her two units of blood. I told her it was "Go Home Juice". I asked her if she wanted me to bring her some lunch and she said, "Taco Bell !" . . . no problemo. I think she is finally getting used to the idea of the colostomy. The colon surgeon came in and removed her staples yesterday and said she looked good. I asked him if she should avoid any types of food for a while and he said no, but food high in fiber can slow things down. Then he laughed. He told us that he had one colostomy patient that loves fresh Indiana corn. Because of his love for fresh corn every August or September he gets a call from the emergency room that his patient has been admitted. Of course the ER doctor panics because he sees a total colon blockage and strongly recommends emergency surgery. Kristen's surgeon says no, just his annual ER run from the fresh Indiana corn! This made Kristen laugh . . . huge progress for her.

Around 6 pm we headed home. It has been a long 2 weeks. The goal now is for her to heal and be able to finish the chemo program she had started, and, if necessary, enroll in the Erbitux clinical trial. Of course, Dad is still looking for a complete healing miracle, but he will settle for one more day with little or no pain.

*   *   *   *

Kristen is half way through the first unit of blood. Then after unit number two, she gets to check out of the hospital. She is zonked out right now, but very excited to get out of here and get a good night's sleep. At home I am sure that Kirk and I will peek in on her while she sleeps, but won't be checking her blood pressure, oxygen level, pulse, temperature and heart rate every four hours.

Kristen has an appointment next Thursday with Dr. F, the home visiting nurse tomorrow, and Dr. P on Tuesday. I am not sure if she will start chemo up again or wait another week. She is getting back her feisty attitude. When Nurse D asked her the other night what his name was, she said "Josh". Then what my name was and she thought and thought and finally said "Linda" . . . freaked us out until she started laughing.

One of our star nurses is D. Brother Eric went to the gift shop and purchased an alligator puppet that had its own little finger puppets with Velcro sticking on the hand of Ali Gator. Nurse D would come to Kristen's room and they put on a puppet show. We noticed that the gift store still had another Ali Gator left so we bought Nurse D his own. We got to see him before we left and gave him his own Ali Gator. I spoke to one of the nurses when we left and she said Nurse D was already using the puppet to bring smiles to others on his floor. When another nurse asked him about the puppet he told her about Kristen and broke down and cried. We can't say enough wonderful things about the nurses and doctors on the oncology floor.

Mom

March 1—Saturday

We got home Thursday night shortly before midnight with Kristen in tow from her seventeen day stay at St Vincent's. She used her walker to get from the van to the house. She fell because her legs were very weak from bed rest, and cried all the way to the bathroom.

Kirk, the light sleeper, slept in the guest room next to Kristen's so he could hear her if she needed something. She is using her walker to get back and forth to the bathroom. We can see major improvements in her mobility today.

She fought nausea and gas pain most of the morning. The home visiting nurse came at noon. Kristen had a hard time getting comfortable most of the day. She tried different sofas. Finally Mom got her back into her bed and slept in a chair next to her. Kristen didn't want to be alone. I can imagine after being in the hospital for 17 days, always having someone there, she wasn't ready to be by herself. She finally got comfortable and slept during the afternoon. Kristen thanked us countless times today.

I bought a baby monitor with a pager button for Kristen's room so we could hear her. It works great. I drove to the Walgreen's pharmacy with a handful of prescriptions. I handed them to our pharmacist . . . . M . . . another angel in our path. I waited for a while and then heard my name called over the paging system. M pushed two large grocery sized bags across the counter to me and with compassion in his voice he asked me . . . "Are you ok with this?" I swallowed hard, looked at the bags and said "I'll take them home, look them over and let you know".

I had to put all 17 drugs on an Excel spreadsheet to keep track of the dosages and times. These included four painkillers, two antibiotics, two anti-seizure, one diuretic, two anti-nausea, one anti-anxiety, one constipation, one anti-coagulant shot, one anti-stomach acid, one anti-gas and one sleeping pill.

A grateful Dad

March 5—Wednesday

Sister Megan participates in the American Cancer Society's Relay for Life in April. The plan originally was to have Kristen go to Orlando and participate with her. But now that Kristen is in her own battle against cancer, she won't be able to. I know this year the Relay will have a special meaning for Megan.

March 10—Monday

Kristen is learning to walk all over again. Because she has babied her right side for so many months and then spent seventeen days in a hospital bed, the muscles in her thigh have atrophied, and must be rebuilt and retrained. This process is painful. She uses her walker frequently.

The biggest problem is her lower and upper intestinal systems have not restarted which means she can't keep much down. The subsequent reduction in calories has rapidly brought her weight down to 116 lbs. The daily bouts of nausea keep her in bed which aggravates the intestinal problems. One problem leads to the next problem to be solved.

After having fought the battle against advanced cancer for 9 long months, a person realizes the numerous ups and downs experienced and how much stamina even the caregivers have to muster.

The good news is that she is using her breakthrough pain control (Oxycodone) rarely. No fever and last week's chemistry results for white cells, hemoglobin, INR (5), and potassium looked very good. With seventeen medications going into her, you would expect her chemistry numbers to be out of tolerance.

March 14—Friday

Kristen had an appointment today with Dr. F. I can't remember the last update that I sent out, so I will try to give a quick recap.

Last Wednesday after Kristen ate dinner. I gave her one of her antibiotics, she vomited. It repeated again on Thursday, breakfast, lunch and dinner. It was the same routine. So we stopped the antibiotics. She slowly has gotten better. But it has been a setback after having a fairly good appetite, she has lost 15 pounds. But she is a petite girl and looks pretty skinny. In fact Dr F said no chemo today, and advised her to gain some weight, and I will see you in two weeks.

She is constipated which makes it uncomfortable to eat. She has been able to keep yogurt, Jell-O, and chicken noodle soup down, but that isn't going to get the weight back on.

Her friends, Chelsea and Chris, came by yesterday and brought her two kittens. It wore Kristen out. Kristen had really been looking forward to seeing her kittens.

Next week, Dr. F wants Kristen to have a PET scan to see what the cancer is doing. Hopefully, the report will show no change from the December 20th scan. Maybe by next week Kristen will have gained a few pounds.

One of my friends from Delaware sent Kristen a T-shirt that says "One Brave Chick" She continues to amaze us with her strength. She does have her down moments and wants to be a normal 23 year-old. We are grateful that she is staying with us and letting us take care of her.

*   *   *   *

Dr F's office called this afternoon and wants Kristen to get potassium in an IV and another blood test.

Three big days in a row for her, she is pretty worn out. Two of Kristen's friends came to visit for a few hours. Our friend C, who is a nurse at Riverview, stopped by to see her on her way home from work.

March 16—Sunday

After episodes of vomiting, losing weight and constipation, Mom and Dad conferenced and decided it was time to call the doctor and head for the hospital, again. Kristen's abdomen was so swollen she looked 8 months pregnant. We took her to the Emergency Room at St. Vincent's. She got a CT scan, and it showed she has a blocked small intestine where it meets the large intestine and was filled with fluid. She also has some fluid in her lungs which can be a breeding ground for pneumonia. She is in ICU for at least two days. They aren't sure how long they will keep her. She is a very sick girl. Her blood chemistry numbers are out of acceptable ranges, potassium extremely low, and her blood acidity way off. All could be life threatening.

The ER doctor pulled Brenda and I into a conference room and asked us if we realized how seriously ill Kristen was. The doctor said "Kristen was dying". Maybe, but what the ER doctor doesn't realize was that a lot of the problems Kristen was experiencing have been around awhile. It still hits you like a ton of rocks. We are holding out hope for a recovery from this pit.

Really need the prayers now, even more.

A grateful Dad

Life is beautiful
fulfilling . . . never empty
only if you allow your eyes to open
all the way
so you can see the wonderful ways of people
the sunshine burns into my arm
skin baking in the sun
how the warmth spreads through
finger tips to my tiny toes
obligations are nothing
slip into our daily routine
slip into darkness
make everyday yours
make it fresh and exciting

—Kristen

Miracle Child

Kristen's best friend Chelsea, Mom and Dad spent the night in ICU. Her best friend Jeff went home at 3 am and was back again at 7 pm. What dedicated and loving friends she has. It really shows what this younger generation is made of, and I like what I see.

We slept in a couple of different ICU lounges. I had one all to myself until 3:45 am when I awoke to see a doctor sitting by himself looking very troubled. I wanted to wake completely and ask him if he was ok, but I couldn't get the strength. Then at 4 am an older lady, her daughter, and son-in-law came in and started discussing someone who had just died. Later I found out it was the gentleman in the ICU room next to Kristen. They were being briefed on the arrangements with the funeral home. I think the doctor was his ICU doctor and he was very troubled by the loss of his patient—more apparent compassion.

Dad

*   *   *   *

How do I say this, a <u>miracle</u> has happened! I tell my children that when modern medicine cannot explain something wonderful that has happened, it was because God stepped in, did his thing and left his signature on it.

Last night we thought we were going to lose Kristen. Blood chemistry, kidney function, oxygen, CO_2, and white count were all bad. Everything was coming unglued fast. I think the ER doctor thought we would lose her in 24 hours and tried to prepare us for it. Early in the morning, I went to her room and brushed a cool, wet washcloth over her forehead and fed her ice. She really liked it. At 6 am a resident came in and said that they had requested a room for Kristen on the Oncology floor. I said, "Huh?" I thought she needed to be watched and was on the borderline? "Well

Mr. Forbes, Kristen's chemistry numbers have all recovered. It has even surprised us and we are releasing her to a regular room."

A few hours later we are on the Oncology floor and the nurses are, once again, wanting to see Kristen. I asked for a copy of Kristen's chemistry numbers when we hit the ER last night and compared them to the most recent ones. They didn't even look like the same person. Last night's chemistry numbers showed a young lady whose systems were being overwhelmed and shut down. But today's were . . . well . . . only the potassium was a little low! This was God answering all the prayers for a miracle. THANK YOU!

Now we wait to see if she will have to undergo surgery to remove the blockage, or if God might work another miracle.

An extremely grateful and overwhelmed Dad

March 18—Tuesday

Dr. F requested a patient consult for Kristen. This made yesterday a very long and stressful day with doctors parading through and giving their opinions. Dr. F was the first in the morning, and he is hoping the stomach tube will take care of the blockage. Then came the infectious disease doctor, who talked about doing a CT scan to insert a needle into the pelvic area to drain. Then the bowel surgeon gave her the "worse case scenario". I will skip the details of that conversation. Then the urologist told us that the kidneys seem to be working fine. Each came with their own specialty, expressing their opinion. Their opinions formed an endless string of bad news for Kristen to absorb which created lots of tears. It was like standing waist deep in the ocean with wave after wave pounding you down until you are on your knees unable to stand up. Then at 6pm she finally had a major emotional meltdown requiring a dose of Ativan to calm her down.

Mom spent the night but got no sleep. About 2 am Kristen came out of the Ativan, pulled out her stomach drain tube (NG) and melted down again. She turned and said to her mother "Don't be mad at me". About 4 am everything quieted down. Dr. F came in about 6:45 am. He pulled up a chair, leaned over the bed, held her hand and spoke to her about her options. He spoke to her like a loving father not a doctor. Long ago we told him we don't view him as her doctor but a member of our family. He said we will continue to empower Kristen to make her own decisions. He said that if we get to the point that there are no more options he will tell us.

The plan now is to get an X-ray of the small intestine and decide if the NG tube to pump out the gastric juices needs to go back in or if a more semi-permanent tube should be implanted directly into the stomach. Radiology would then put a needle into her pelvis and drain off the abscess if Kristen decides to do it. They will probably install a PICC line into her upper arm vein for nutrients. Poor kid . . . she is starved. She needs to get her weight back on. Hydrating with the IV fluids is making her look so much better.

I think the best prayers now are for wisdom for Kristen to make the best decisions for her future and that God gives his peace to her and her family to accept the decisions she makes.

A very grateful Dad,

March 19—Wednesday

Dr. F came in and talked with Kristen. The X-ray showed there is still a small bowel obstruction . . . so no food. He would like to have her get a PowerPort (7), so she can get nutrition through it. It will be used for chemo, blood work, and fluids. She will not have to get poked and prodded any more and won't need further major surgery. He wants her to get the weight back on, grow stronger and start chemo. Radiology told Dr. F that they don't want to implant the needle into the abscess because it could cause a hole that wouldn't close up. Dr. F was concerned about her calcium numbers and wants to have a bone scan and skeletal survey. Fortunately, the guy from Nuclear that came to give her the injection for the bone scan was the same person that had done her PET scans. This made it a little easier for her. She is still overwhelmed with all that is going on. But the good news is that stuff is at last shuffling through her digestive tract. She had me change her Ostomy bag two times today. Wouldn't it be great if this small bowel obstruction miraculously disappears?

Yesterday, she was an emotional wreck. Every 2 hours she got up to go to the bathroom. I had to get up, unplug the electric cord for her IV stand and wait for her. Then get her back in bed, cover her up, and talk to her while she cried. All day yesterday, it was information overload. All the doctors trying to explain what they want done. They all want it done yesterday. We decided "Enough!"

Kirk told Kristen "We are now on your time. You make the decisions. You can set one goal of what you want to do each day". At 5 this morning she asked me what I thought she should have as her goal. I told her after Dr. F talks to you, you can set your goal. One of them was to walk the hallway. She didn't get that done because two tests took several hours and wore her out.

She let me help her with her physical therapy this evening instead of walking. I don't think she is up to walking the hallway with other people watching her. After all, she is 23 and those wonderful hospital gowns. She did have a couple of her friends stop by this evening. Meghan from the ER came bearing flowers, and Steve shared words of encouragement. He told her how strong and brave she is. He didn't think that he could do what she is doing. God always knows when to send the right people every day for what Kristen needs.

We called the pain doctor yesterday morning. He wasn't aware she was in the hospital. So he has adjusted her pain meds and it was so much better today. She still has her meltdowns but she is such a strong young lady.

Thank you for your continued prayers and always thinking of Kristen. She said several times today that she wishes this was a bad dream and she would wake up. Pray that the bone scan comes back fine and she will be ready to get the PowerPort put in and start getting nutrition into her. She is allowed to eat only ice chips.

March 20—Thursday

The good news for today is the bone scan and the skeletal survey were negative! It was pretty scary waiting for results for what could have been bone cancer. Kristen signed the surgery consent to implant the PowerPort. I am sure once it is in, she will wonder why she waited this long. Kristen went for a walk down the hall to the lounge today. The journey wore her out. She let me help her with her physical therapy to relieve some pain.

Last week <u>The Bee Movie</u> was released and Blockbuster was selling the DVD along with a set of bee antenna to wear on your head. I bought one for Kristen and took it to the hospital to entertain everyone. Hopefully, I would put a smile on Kristen's face. I wore the antenna down the hallway to the nurse's station and buzzed them saying that "We need to BEE happy and BEE positive so all the patients can BUZZ out of here and go home soon." Everyone laughed and agreed to do their best. A few days later, one of the nurses said she had a difficult patient and asked if she could borrow the bee antenna. She put on a clean room outfit, which is special clothing that is bright yellow with black trim, a pair of sanitary goggles and gloves topped off with my bee antenna. It brought laughs to the entire hall. Even the "difficult" patient laughed. Mission accomplished!

Last night was a long night. Kristen was up every hour on the hour. At 2 am she wanted her Dad. Kristen got scared and had a pain-control issue so Nurse D put the bee antenna on, spread out his arms like a plane and buzzed the room saying he was her Dad buzzing in to see her. He got her laughing and refocused.

I know she is anxious about surgery tomorrow.   at
time it will happen. They will either put her all the   y
sedate her. Her mood swings don't seem to be as bad

March 22—Saturday

Kristen had her PowerPort installed below her left shoulder bone. They will run all the IVs, nutrition, and chemo, through it and draw blood for testing, all without sticking her arms. She has been a difficult and painful stick.

This was the fifth time for being under for a surgery or procedure since July. She did extremely well. Pain is still under control and her mood swings are milder. The goal for today is to start feeding her nutrients, TPN **(8),** through her new PowerPort to build her strength and send her home. Then she can finish the chemo she started a month ago which was interrupted by the infection caused by the leaky bowel.

After Mom had spent a full week at her bedside, I stood watch and sent Mom home for a few hours to shower and boil Easter eggs. Kristen said she wanted to dye eggs for Easter. The nurses always have an Easter Parade with costumes on Easter weekend.

While Brenda was gone, Kristen awoke from a nap and looked at me with those beautiful blue eyes and said, "Dad, I am going to heaven". I was surprised at her statement and looked at her and said "I know . . . are you planning on leaving soon?" She said "No". I thought about it for a moment and said "Kristen, will you promise me something? Will you promise me that if you get there before I do that you will stand at the gate and wait for me?" She smiled and said "Sure Dad, I will wait at the gate for you" and she went back to sleep.

Oh dear God this is so hard.

Eric and Jamie helped Kristen dye Easter eggs. Kristen asked Eric to dump the leftover blue dye in her urine pail in the toilet to surprise the nurse. The nurse went in to measure the urine and there was a pregnant pause. The nurse tried to figure out what in the world was wrong with Kristen that would produce blue urine. Finally she got the joke and laughed. We all laughed. On Easter, Eric, Jeff and Mom snuck Kristen off the 6th floor in a wheelchair with her bunny ears on. They took her to the lobby so she could enjoy looking outdoors.

Thanks for all the prayers.

A very grateful Dad

March 25—Tuesday

At 6 this morning Dr. F came in bright and early with his usual flipping on the lights and his "Good morning Princess!" He told Kristen we would wait until tomorrow to implant the infection drain. Dad will be back in town. This greatly relieved Kristen. Her friend Jeff came and spent the night and stayed all day.

She was awake more today and it appears that her energy level is improving. The nutrition bag runs through her PowerPort for 24 hours. It has 1,500 calories. Kristen tried playing games on the computer. She made a dot to dot game and had to teach Jeff how to play. This afternoon she taught me how to play a card game and the three of us played cards for over an hour. Her sense of humor was back too. She is still hungry and ice chips don't cut it.

March 26—Wednesday

I got back in town. Brenda took a break and stepped out. Kristen woke for a moment and said "Dad, I had a funny dream, I dreamed of Grandma Porter" (deceased) . . . I said . . ."What did she say?" Kristen said, "Nothing, but she had a peg leg." I asked her what do you think the spiritual message was in that? She said "I don't know but I have been dreaming about Grandma Porter a lot".

I believe that God sends someone you have had a close, loving relationship with to bring you home to heaven when life ends.

I don't like this.

Dad

PS . . . I later looked up on the Internet to see if the peg leg is symbolic anywhere. I found that Joe Peg Leg was one sign used in the Civil War to show slaves a way home to freedom from slavery. Was God telling Kristen that he was about to show her a way home?

March 27—Thursday

Today Kristen went back for another CT scan. I missed the meeting with Dr. F to see what it was for, so we wait. Kristen received two units of blood last night. What a difference a couple of units of blood and nutrition can make. She has been awake all day today, shampooed and straightened her hair, sat in a chair for couple hours, and has colored in coloring books. New person . . . I hope it lasts. Now we need her to be able to eat, something she hasn't done for a month.

Yesterday was a long, stressful day. Kristen was scheduled for a CT scan with contrast fluid. They were late to transport her to X-ray. Once again, Kristen had the NG tube put in, something she hated. Dr. F told her the tube wouldn't be in very long. After they put the tube in, they started the fluid. Unfortunately, the contrast fluid moved very slowly down into her small intestine. This caused a delay of another hour and another x-ray. It happened again and again. Finally the CT tech came in and took her for her CT scan. When they brought her back, she still had the NG tube. It hadn't been removed. Kristen got back to her room after six hours. The delay was no fault of the medical staff. The fluid simply moved very slowly. Her nurses were even worried something had happened since we were gone for so long. After Kristen was back in her room, she had another emotional meltdown. She was mad the tube was still in and "if it isn't out in ten minutes she is personally removing it". So Dad leaps into action. He hunts down a nurse to call Dr F's office. Dr. F tells the nurses to take the tube out. This improved her mood somewhat, but she was still upset that she had been in X-ray for almost six hours.

March 28—Friday

This morning, Dr. F came in and said there is a partial small bowel obstruction, but for right now she wouldn't need surgery. She can start with small amounts of liquids, since it will take longer for it to move through. I think that was a positive thing for her to hear. We didn't tell him that she had been sneaking tea for the last three days and wasn't having a problem unless she drank too much. He wants to see how the liquids go, before she can take another step up the food chain.

He talked about her going home next week. The nutrition (TPN) will accompany her home. She is thankful that she had the PowerPort put in. She no longer has to endure being stuck in another vein to start a new IV. Everything can go through her PowerPort.

Kirk has talked with her about giving up her apartment. He wants her to look at it as a temporary thing. When she is stronger and back on her feet, her furniture can come out of storage and into a new place for her to live. The plan is on Sunday to load up her furnishings in a U-Haul and put most of them in a storage unit. Her bedroom furniture will come to our house. She isn't happy about it, but knows it's the right decision. Jeff is lining up friends to help move on Sunday. He is going to take care of her cats. She is really homesick for them and misses them a lot. Kristen realizes she needs to have people looking out for her all the time now.

Several of the nurses have told us that Kristen has the "A" team of doctors. God placed the best in her path. If a nurse hasn't been on duty for a few days, they always come to see Kristen to get the latest update.

March 30—Sunday

Yesterday was the second good day in a row. We got Kristen to walk down the hall and circle the nurses' station. Then we went down the hall to the lounge where she sat at a table. She looked up at me with those beautiful blue eyes and said "Dad, go get the cards" Say what? "Let's play cards" Ok. For the next two hours Eric, Megan, Kristen and I played cards. I was astounded . . . that is the first time she has done this in several months.

A very, very grateful Dad

April 3—Thursday

Kristen had an MRI to see if they could find the problem causing her right leg to swell again. She has her sense of humor along with her quick wit. The MRI transporter, A, knows Kristen well now. After we loaded her on the transport gurney, Kristen held her arms out like she was Superman flying off for her MRI, so A hummed the Superman theme song. Ali Gator her hand puppet was along for the ride. We, the Princess' entourage, laughed all the way to MRI.

Thank you all for your prayers, cards, flowers, and stuffed animals. Kristen received a Moose with a broken leg today from one of Kirk's friends. She is sleeping with Ali Gator on one side and Moose on the other. Keep praying for her to regain her stamina and get back on chemo.

The doctors are saying the end of this hospital stay is near. She is holding down the pills given to her so far. I revised the Excel spreadsheet that covers all the meds and their dosages. She took a shower yesterday and was up from about 11 am to 5 pm . . . longest run since I can remember. She had the occupational therapist and the physical therapist evaluate her. She did some drawings, played with Play Do, drank fluids, ate Jell-O, drank tea, and I slipped her a Hershey Kiss candy when the nurse wasn't looking, and it stayed down. She will be going home with a nutrition (TPN) bag periodically attached to her PowerPort. This will continue until she can eat by mouth. I think she is ready to go home.

One great story happened yesterday. We have been trying to get a good supplier for her Ostomy supplies. Most drugstores don't carry them. I finally talked to Walgreens. The pharmacist has been a great help to me since this all began. He said he would fax the product list to one of their two pharmacies which can get the supplies. I called him last night to follow up and he had gone home. His coworker said he had faxed it to their New Castle, IN store to see what they could do. I called the New Castle office and the man on the phone said "Is this for Kristen Forbes, who is a Walgreens' employee?" I said, "Uh, yes but she is out on medical leave." He said "My name is S, I know your daughter. I worked with her in the Carmel store." I said, "Oh, yes, I remember meeting you when I picked up something for Kristen once." He said "Well, sir, I am the manager here now and I will personally get these supplies arranged for you, plus I will drive them up to Noblesville because I don't live far away. You will have them Friday night". I was speechless. I can't wait to tell Kristen that God had intervened again on her behalf. I must have told him thank you several times.

Thank you for your prayers, as you can see they are working incredible miracles for Kristen. I think I could write a book on them.

A very grateful and thankful Dad

*   *   *   *

We never imagined that we would have to absorb so much medical knowledge in such a short period of time. We are now learning about TPN which Kristen will be on for her nutritional needs. They want her to be on it from 8pm until 8am. It would give her freedom during the daytime hours. We aren't sure how long she will use the TPN. It will be in a "Kangaroo" backpack which will hold the TPN nutrition bag, tubing and a battery powered pump. The backpack can be placed at her bedside so she can easily move during the night.

April 4 6:45am—Friday

We can hear Dr. F coming down the hallway

If I can prove I'm fine without the pain pump, I can go home today! So hopefully my meds will pan out.

April 5 Saturday

TPN IV through PowerPort instructions by the nurse.

Relaxing
just as the sun sets
then I find time
to come to terms with myself

The beat vibrates
touches my toes
shakes me into reality
something that
everyone can be touched by

Move back and forth
don't ask why
follow what you feel
and what you want to do
by day's end you'll feel
much better

Come with me
let me show you something
show you how the world is
wonderful

—Kristen

Home

April 6—Sunday

Brenda woke up at 3:50 am and unhooked her TPN nutrition bag. By 9 am Kristen was going through her moving boxes in her room, organizing and sorting her things. She took a shower and washed her hair. She told us she is doing a lot better than people are giving her credit for. The girls put together puzzles and watched a couple of movies. She went all day and stayed up late.

I don't understand what is happening but I can't say thank you enough. What a gift from God. Whether it is permanent or only short term, I will savor every minute of it and say thanks.

A grateful, beyond expression, Dad

I got a text message from Kristen . . . her friend Jeff had to go to the Custard Stand and make vanilla custard this afternoon, so Kristen went there with him and propped up her swollen leg. She feels great, no pain, and even sampled some mint chocolate chip custard.

April 7 Monday

Home Nurse's Visit

Weight 124 lbs.

When she walked in, she said that I looked amazing.

Blood Pressure was 123 over 80. Yea!

She took 2 vials of blood.

<u>April 8 Tuesday</u>

To Do List:

Jeff's house . . . . to play with Kitties

Trade Secret . . . . Set up appt to get hair trimmed and highlights

National City Bank . . . Cash in change rolled with Mom

JC Penny . . . 20% off Bedding

Lowe's . . . 10% off, want to buy seeds and starter kits for my garden

Wal-Mart . . . toothbrushes

Michaels . . . . Scrapbook stuff

April 9—Wednesday

I still don't understand but I will gratefully accept what is going on with Kristen.

Day 3: At home . . . kicked back that day, took naps, rolled her spare change and came up with $200. She wants to go and get her hair done tomorrow with the cash. Her leg is still swollen, but overall she is doing great.

Day 4: Spent the morning organizing her "stuff" and went to her storage unit for more "stuff". Her best friend Chelsea came over at noon, and picked Kristen up. She had a borrowed wheelchair in her car just in case. They went to Jeff's house to see Kristen's cats. She spent two hours playing with them. Then, like all good ladies would, headed out to go shopping and came home around 9pm.

April 10—Thursday

I submitted Kristen's application for Social Security Disability. I used a website developed by a former Social Security caseworker. He shows how to properly fill out the forms and how to use the correct wording for the application. Many people told me it would take 12-18 months to get an approval.

April 10—Thursday

I dropped her off at Jeff's. Jacob was there. If it is not raining they are going to his first T-Ball practice. He was pretty excited. Jacob gave me a huge bear hug. Kristen will call when she wants me to pick her up.

The physical therapist and home nurse came today. Nurse J changed her PowerPort access, drew blood and checked blood pressure. The therapist reevaluated her and showed her exercises she could use to jump start the lymph system. She watched her walk and couldn't believe how well she did. The leg swelling is down today.

April 10 Thursday

I took 2mg of Oxycodone around 4:30pm. Slept all day yesterday, so I didn't have a Wednesday. Today I came over to Jeff's, to see Jacob and of course my kitties. Jacob was supposed to have his first T-ball post and bats. It was cancelled because of the rain.

April 12—Saturday

I landed at Indianapolis Airport last evening and had a text message from Brenda saying a local Italian restaurant had delivered supper courtesy of the Kuhl Family.

I got home, walked into the house and the aroma of Italian food and fresh Italian bread hit me . . . yum! Sat down with Brenda and had the most wonderful meal in a long time . . . one hosted by a good friend and former college roommate. Oh . . . the salad . . . the main course . . . the fresh bread . . . and . . . oh yes the delectable dessert pastries . . . YUM! What a nice way to arrive home after seven days on the road eating "road meals". This was like home cooking! The best part was that there was enough for two families, so we froze the leftovers and, trust me, will be enjoying this meal several times before I go back on the road again in five days. Eric is coming home from Purdue this weekend so he will enjoy the meal also.

Brenda and I cannot thank you enough. This was a very special gift that will be remembered for a lifetime.

From the Forbes Family to the Kuhl Family . . . from deep in our hearts . . .

Thank you.

<u>April 12—Saturday</u>

Sometimes it leaves me awe struck how the love of friends floods over you when you need the encouragement to go one more day in a battle against something as serious as cancer. God steps in and gives you the strength needed, through your friends. Just to mention some of things that have happened over the last few weeks . . . A good Ohioan friend sent Kristen a "wounded moose" stuffed animal all the way from Maine to cheer her up in the hospital. It worked. Lots of cards, flowers and phone calls from all over the country . . . even emails from friends as far away as Bolivia. Another friend sent her two stuffed cats that are the same colors as her real cats so she can enjoy them while she is separated from her cats. Last night I sat down with Brenda and had the most wonderful meal in a long time.

Kristen continues to do very well. The biggest problem right now is the swollen right leg which is caused by lymphedema (9). It can be painful and hard to treat. We are trying MLD massage which is Manual Lymph Drainage to stimulate drainage of the lymph system back into areas of the body that can easily absorb the excess fluid. The physical therapist seems to think Kristen should be able to leap this hurdle too. Both the visiting nurse and the therapist said they are surprised how well Kristen is doing. I came home from the road and saw a new person. She had her hair highlighted and trimmed and looks really cute. She sat on a chair in the kitchen and did her nails last night. Of course, she wants her Dad to do her toenails since he did such an outstanding job in the hospital last time. Maybe I could make this my retirement career?

A grateful and pleasantly surprised Dad

<u>April 15—Tuesday</u>

The very active week and higher narcotics caught up with her. This week she came to a roaring stop. She is very tired and sleeps 70% of the day. Yesterday we decided to be proactive again and called Dr. P, the pain doctor, who was on vacation when she was released from the hospital. He moved her back to the levels she was originally on. Now we wait and see if the baseline pain protection is high enough.

The physical therapist comes three times a week to stimulate her lymph system and work her legs to fight the swelling. The visiting nurse comes twice a week to check vitals, draw blood and change her PowerPort. Nurse Brenda and Nurse Kirk have been prepping and plugging in her overnight nutrition pump (TPN), which comes in a backpack so you can travel with it. It is very convenient. Today's technology is mind bending and beautiful.

Dr. F wants her to come in next week to restart chemo. Hopefully, this will shrink the tumor to get pressure off her small bowel so she can eat again. We ordered Chinese carryout from down the street and Kristen ate the egg drop soup and sucked the filling out of the crab rangoon. What a trooper. She hardly ever complains and makes a parent very proud.

A grateful Dad,

Nurse Kirk

April 18—Friday

Kristen is still sleeping at least 16 hours a day. We lowered her base pain medicine which made her more alert. We got her outside on a lounge chair yesterday for about 15 mins. I told her she could soak up some of that wonderful spring day warmth and the Sun's vitamin E. You could tell she really enjoyed it. She is consuming about 600 calories of drinks on top of the 1500 calories in her nutrition bag. She has appointments next week and maybe a restart of the chemo program she was in before the infection setback in January.

Now for the really interesting thing: About four days ago I went into her room and found her sitting on the floor in the corner of her room next to a dresser. She was writing some notes. I looked at her and said, "What are you doing over there?" She said she was there because everything in the room moved almost a foot. I said "Like an earthquake?" She said "Yes". I blew it off thinking it was all the drugs she was on and probably a dream. Well, if you saw the news today, you would know that Indiana had a 5.2 magnitude earthquake today. I know . . . I know . . . but it happened.

April 22-Tuesday

Dr. P

Increase breakthrough to 15mg pills

April 24—Thursday

Kristen had an appointment with Dr. F yesterday. No chemo, not strong enough. Her hemoglobin was down too. We went to Riverview

Hospital and spent from noon until 10:30 pm while she received her two bags of blood and a drug that takes the calcium from your blood and puts it back into your bones. Her calcium level was a little high and that can cause kidney failure if not stopped.

Dr. F said it was decision time. Kristen needs to decide whether she wants more chemo or to stop the treatment. I wasn't expecting that conversation. Kristen was really tired and fighting to stay awake when she saw Dr. F. I don't think this whole topic soaked in because she never said anything about it the rest of the day. It is not going to be easy to bring this topic up again. I told him we would let him know next week.

Tough time, lots of tears.

A very tired Dad

April 28—Monday

Her Physical Therapist, who Kristen calls her Personal Trainer, had wrapped her swollen legs Thursday. Today she removed the wraps to analyze the fluid reduction. She said "Her legs looked amazingly good". She will do one more wrap sequence to reduce more fluid then will size Kristen for custom pressure stockings. In the past the extreme swelling would cause considerable pain and discomfort. We had to massage her leg to drain her lymph system. During the last four "wrapped" days she has not complained once about discomfort caused by the swelling or the tightly wrapped legs.

An old problem surfaced again, she started filling up with the liquid. It was almost like the small bowel obstruction had closed down again and we thought we were headed for the emergency room. This time Mom and Dad interceded and limited her intake to ice chips and a few drinks. After about 48 hours she was fine and things were moving through her again and she was keeping everything down.

Friday she spent visiting her cats at Jeff's house. Yesterday she walked out to the kitchen in the morning and told me she wanted to get out of the house for a while, so we went to Lowe's and bought garden seeds. We decided we would plant our first garden in almost 10 years just for Kristen. We are going to plant it near the house windows, so if she can't go outside she can at least watch it grow through the windows. Then we went to Kohl's and she spent some of her tax rebate for clothes and a ring. After a nap, her brother Eric helped her to plant the seeds in small pots. Today, her brother (who is home to study for finals at Purdue) took her to Meijers with Mom. Eric pushed her around the store in her wheel chair. She bought scrapbook materials, more seeds, and found the clearance aisle with picture frames. It is moments like these and last summer when sister Megan came home from Orlando for four weeks to care for her sister, that make you proud.

May 1—Thursday

We said goodbye to home nurse J today. J is retiring after three decades of nursing. She gave Kristen a hug and told her she was going to keep praying for her. I walked out with her and told her about Dr F and the conversation last week. She said Kristen should definitely do the chemo. She has come such a long way and is doing well. The physical therapist came to visit at the same time. Since last Friday, Kristen has lost 8 cm in right leg and 6 cm in the left leg. She said it was amazing. Normally she doesn't see that much difference in just a week's time. They were impressed.

May 3—Saturday

The fluid buildup caught up with Kristen and she threw up several times. Brenda called me in Chicago and said they were headed for the emergency room. I drove home through thunderstorms that were so bad that I had to pull off the Interstate three times. Once we came to a dead stop, and the semi behind me started hydroplaning and almost jack knifed. As I watched this in the rearview mirror, all I could think about was how late this accident was about to make me or worse. But the trucker was skilled enough to get it stopped and not park his truck in my rear seat.

When Eric and Brenda got her to the ER last night, she was dehydrated. They started her on fluids, and after the first bag she was feeling better. Jeff rushed to join us in the ER. Pain didn't become a problem until 1 am. They gave her a shot of Dilaudid. Eric and I headed for home around 1:30 am and Brenda spent the night with her.

Kristen had a CT scan. The blockage hasn't changed from the CT scan five weeks ago. There are also a couple spots on her lungs. The doctors said it may be cancer. Later, I ran into Dr. D who had looked over her test results and said it could even be infection. The infectious disease doctor thought the blockage didn't look as bad as five weeks ago. The urologist came in and said both kidney's are enlarged. Kristen will have her right stent in her ureter replaced and they will put one in her left ureter.

Last week, one of the founders of Dr. D's medical group made his annual pilgrimage to Lourdes, France, the site of many healing miracles. He has one patient that he focuses on each year. This year it was Kristen. He had all her medical updates and a photo of her. He gave it to one of the Bauds, who took it into the holy water and prayed for healing. We will take all the Divine help we can get.

We continue to be amazed at how many lives Kristen's illness has touched. One of our neighbors, who is a doctor, told me that it has changed the way he talks to parents of young girls about the HPV vaccine.

May 7—Wednesday

This morning they surgically replaced the stent in her right side ureter tube and placed another in her left side. The chemistry numbers on her kidneys were starting to deteriorate. Hopefully she will get to go home tomorrow if she gets her pain under control.

We haven't gotten a copy of her blood labs to see what her numbers look like, especially the hemoglobin. Since it has only been a week, that number should still be okay. Her numbers looked good in the emergency room, which was a huge sigh of relief.

Since the President asked us to spend our tax rebate to fire up the economy, we got Kristen a Wii game console and assorted games. She asked for one at Christmas but I said "I'm not putting that kind of money into a video game." Circumstances change and so do attitudes, so we invested in a Wii™ system. Wow, what a game system. Eric and I tried it out at home and bowled, boxed, baseballed, golfed, air hockeyed and raced late into the night. We took it to the hospital and hooked it into Kristen's room TV and even the doctors and nurses are coming in to check it out. What fun! We even got Dr. D to write Kristen a prescription for a Wii system to "be used only under a doctor's close supervision and participation".

Thanks for all the prayers . . . they sure got us through this trip (the 3rd) to the Emergency Room . . . at least we spent no time in the ICU.

A grateful Dad

*   *   *   *

Kristen had a really rough day at the hospital yesterday. Pain was out of control to the point where she couldn't walk even two steps to the bathroom without crying. I really thought we were going to be stuck in the hospital for the long haul. But like many times before God steps in and says "Watch this!"

I got Kristen's new prescriptions for her return home and headed down to the hospital. Mom spent all night with Kristen. I could tell on the phone the evening had not gone well. By the time I got to the hospital,

Kristen was sitting on the edge of the bed saying she was going home. So we did. We got her settled in about 4 pm. Since then she has been up watching TV with her brother and some friends. Her pain doctor (they are worth their weight in gold) had adjusted her pain medication and she is doing very well. The big concern now is her kidneys. The numbers are not looking very good. We are hoping the new kidney stents will help.

More good stories . . . we were so burned out on this hospital stay that we came home forgetting her walker, which is like cutting her off at the knees. She can't walk very well yet, so Dad calls the nurse's station on Kristen's floor. They locate the walker and tag it for somebody to pick up. I knew I would have to go get it because she wouldn't be able to function without it. Then a thought . . . call her friend Meghan, who works nights in the Emergency Room and hope she is working. She calls me back and says she is leaving the hospital after a class. She becomes an angel and says she will go up to the 6th floor and will bring the walker to our house. I see a car pull up to the house. Thinking it was Meghan, I go out to greet her. Up the driveway walks a very tired man carrying a grocery size bag and hands it to me. He says that was a long drive. I said "Thanks, this is my sick daughter's food." He said he had driven it all the way from Chicago to Indianapolis (3 hours). He delivers for a Chicago company who custom produces individualized TPN (nutrition) bags for patients and usually FedEx's them. But because of the last minute dismissal from the hospital they had his delivery service drive it all the way to us. I told him he was an angel and this food is critical for my daughter's survival. I think he was moved by how important his delivery had suddenly become. Even the unsuspecting can be enlisted as angels on short notice. We saw two in a few hours. Meghan showed up with Kristen's walker a few minutes later.

Thanks again for all the prayers. They sure helped us get through this hospital run.

A very thankful Dad

May 14—Wednesday

She has been home almost a week, and the pain she experienced in her right leg and hip is still there. Dr P has increased her pain medication and hopefully she will be more comfortable.

The nurse called today from Dr F's office about her blood lab that was drawn today. Her hemoglobin is down to 5.9 (9.0 is minimum). So we are off in the morning to spend the day at Riverview hospital for another two units of blood. Hopefully, it will boost her energy level because she has been pretty sleepy the last couple of days. I think the low number surprised us. We hadn't noticed the loss of color in her face, which we usually have seen.

On Thursday afternoon she has an appointment with Dr. F. Just pray that she is going to be strong enough to start kicking this cancer in the butt again. The appointment is late in the afternoon and don't know if she is up for chemo.

It is great to have Eric home for the summer too. He and Kristen have been hanging out watching TV together in the evenings in her room. As soon as Megan is done teaching school in Orlando, she will be driving back to Indiana to spend some time with her sister. She finished turning in her last teacher's training assignment and is now a certified teacher.

Keep praying for pain-free days. It is wonderful when she is lying in bed and experiencing a pain level of 2 on a scale of 1-10. It is a different story when she gets up to use the bathroom. There have been lots of tears this week on the bathroom trek and getting back in bed waiting for the pain to subside. I bought her a bedside commode so she wouldn't have to walk as far and a new four-wheeled walker with hand brakes and a seat.

May . . . Kristen's Prayer List

Taylor from NC who has been on the transplant list for a while, this is the 2nd time.

Barb, Dad's friend and coworker has breast cancer

Those who are putting their life on the line to protect our freedom!

Mike's journey to California this Friday and his mother who is a breast cancer survivor

Barb and Lisa's traveling around the country

Sarah's cousin's husband's father passed away

Kelly's Mom's health

May . . . . Kristen's "Movies to Buy" List

Face-off
Hitchhiker's Guide to the Galaxy
Aladdin
Bedknobs and Broomsticks

Button Wars
From Dusk till Dawn
Empire
The Jetsons

<u>May 15 Thursday</u>

Kristen's Last Journal Entry

Checkup with Dr. F. Mom and Dad are here with me. Picked Rhododendron and lilacs when leaving the house.

Questions . . .

Why are my ears plugging up randomly?
What signs are you looking for . . . PET scan after chemo is over

<u>May 16—Friday</u>

Prayers were answered big time in the last few days. The pain doctor increased her Oxycotin and it seems to be helping. There are fewer tears. She can't walk except for a few steps, so we have to transport her by wheelchair. At least the bedside commode has eliminated the trek to the bathroom.

She got two units of blood two days ago and her energy level roared back. Visiting nurse came in about 11am yesterday to change her PowerPort. She stayed awake afterwards and then took a shower and spiffed up for Dr. F's visit at 3:45 pm. She even put on makeup. I had told her that if she shows up like last time, half coherent and fighting to stay awake, Dr. F would look at her and say, "No more chemo". Well, she obviously took my words to heart. Not only did she spiff up for the visit, as I took her out the front door in her wheelchair, she picked a bouquet of lilacs and rhododendrons for him. The wonderful aroma of the lilacs filled first our car and then his office. It must have seemed strange to the other people in the waiting room to see Kristen in her wheelchair holding flowers. The lilac purple color even matched Dr. F's tie. Dr. F was impressed. He said to Kristen, "You look great. Have you decided what you want to do?" Kristen looked him in the eyes, smiled and said "More chemo!" So hopefully, next Friday we restart the last chemo regimen of two weeks on, one off, two on, one off and then a PET scan.

It gets better. On the way home she calls her best friend Chelsea and says "I need to get out of the house." Chelsea came over and we maneuvered Kristen into her Mustang as a passenger. Off they went to shop at the crafts store. We told her she needed to be home at a decent hour so I could plug in her TPN (food) bag. Brenda took her first break in eleven months and headed to southern Indiana for a Girl Scout Jamboree over the weekend and left Dad to play full-time nurse. At least I have brother Eric to help.

I forgot to mention, last night with the added energy level, Brenda, Kristen, Eric and I went bowling . . . no . . . not at the real lanes, but on Kristen's new Wii game system. Kristen would lie on the couch and fling her bowling ball down the lane while reclined. It was a blast. We laughed and jumped, those of us who could, as if we were at the real bowling alley. What fun.

Once again, many thanks for all the prayers . . . they worked.

A very, very grateful Dad

May 23—Friday

Thanks for the prayers, they worked again. Kristen was anxious to get the chemo started again so it was no trouble getting her up and moving. After her chemo session, we stopped to get her a frozen Mountain Dew to sooth her mouth. We got her home onto the couch, where she fell asleep. That was four hours ago, and she is still sleeping peacefully.

Because of the pain meds she takes, she has dry mouth. I called our wonderful pharmacist at Walgreens and he had what she needed, liquid saliva. It works great and comes in flavors. We jokingly called it "Spit in a Bottle". Unfortunately, it satisfied the need so well that she wasn't drinking as much liquids, which caused her to become dehydrated.

Our hope is that God will strengthen her body enough to tolerate this treatment and that it works.

A father filled with hope and expectation

*   *   *   *

I took her outside yesterday afternoon and she seemed to enjoy it. She asked me to rub her shoulders and it was so difficult. There is nothing but bones at the base of her neck and shoulders. This is tough.

A grateful Dad

May 24—Saturday

What an incredible young lady she is. The day after chemo, especially with the cocktail they are giving her, you hold your breath and hope things don't come apart at the seams. Today was so dramatically different than the last four days where she had to fight to stay awake, let alone doing anything beyond that. But today was, well what can I say . . . <u>miraculous</u>. I awoke at 5:30 am and listened for her on the monitor and nothing. Normally, we are awakened around 3:00 am with moaning, requests for breakthrough medication and ice packs for her hip. This morning there was nothing, so I got up and peeked in her room and she is sitting on the edge of the bed. I asked her how she was doing, while I fought the urge to ask her if she wanted breakthrough medication. She said she was fine and requested some ice water. I stayed up with her. She flipped on her TV around 7 am and we watched a three hour movie. I think I napped at least once in the chair, but I didn't hear any moaning or requests for medication until 10:30 am.

Brenda told me Kristen had said she wanted to go shopping for scrapbook material. We loaded up Kristen and her wheelchair and the three of us went shopping. We got back around 4 pm and Kristen went to work organizing her bathroom and her new scrapbook material. Now it is 10 pm and the kid is still running strong. We plugged in her TPN (food) bag and she is settled in for the night.

When her Oncologist told me almost a year ago to look for the little miracles along the journey, I know what he meant. Today was one of those miracles, whether it lasts only today or if it is the beginning of something good.

Thanks for the prayers,

A very pleased Dad

May 30—Friday

Kristen received round two of her chemo Wednesday. The only apparent side effect so far was abdominal cramping on round one. Kristen has a hard time walking with the pain in her right leg, so she uses a wheelchair. I am hoping the chemo will help relieve the pain. I was gone most of the week. Brenda said she didn't ask for her breakthrough pain medication very often. Hopefully the chemo is working.

Kristen received two bags of fluid. The drugs she takes, the TPN and chemo, all cause dehydration. Because her hemoglobin is low again she had a blood transfusion. The TPN (food) pharmacy in Chicago saw that she was dehydrated by her chemistry numbers so they have adjusted her TPN and have added a liter of saline solution in the TPN bag each night. This doubled the amount of fluid she gets each night. I am sure this will help her.

After we finished the transfusion at the hospital, Jeff took her to his house so she could spend time with her cats. She was cute. She looked at me with those big beautiful blue eyes and asked if it was ok to go to Jeff's. I said sure as long as you are home at a decent hour. Well about 11:30 pm she gets home. It is 1 am by the time everyone gets to bed. I am glad she is enjoying it.

Thanks for the prayers.

A very grateful Dad

What do I enjoy the most
green grass and blue sky
these pages represent my
life so you should take that
into consideration while
you read what's inside
for what a person has inside is the most private
personal belonging one
may possess

—Kristen

Final Ride

Today Kristen got what she always wanted, a ride in an ambulance with the siren going. Kristen called me into her room to help her get to her bedside commode. This time though she couldn't sit up on her own. I pulled her into a sitting position and she was having difficulty breathing. I laid her on the bed and told Brenda to call 911. I noticed lots of blood on the bed. The local fire department sent an ambulance and two fire trucks. The EMTs put Kristen on a gurney and transported her to the hospital. When we got to the emergency room her blood pressure was only 75/35. E, one of the EMTs, stayed a couple extra hours to help make sure Kristen was comfortable in the emergency room, another life touched by Kristen. The OBGYN doctor, who was called in to help, has a daughter who played in the high school orchestra with Kristen. I knew God had selected him for a reason . . . . his daughter went to school with Kristen and was diagnosed with a serious brain tumor the same month Kristen was diagnosed with cervical cancer. His daughter is in remission. He stayed around a long time to insure Kristen was comfortable. He even came in early the next morning to check on her and see how we were doing.

We called Megan in Orlando and told her to get on the first plane in the morning and fly home to be with Kristen. They kept her comfortable all night in the ICU. We kept vigil with her best friends Jeff and Chelsea. During the night Kristen was indirectly telling us she was leaving . . . . for good. She told her Mom four times she wanted to go "home". Brenda says in retrospect she now knows Kristen was talking about heaven, not our home. Another time she started reaching out toward the ceiling. We asked what she wanted. She was reaching up toward the operating table overhead light . . . . We asked her . . . "Do you want the light?" She shook her head yes, so we pulled it down near her. We did not realize she was talking about the shining light only she could see . . . the light of Christ coming to get her.

<u>June 1 Sunday</u>

Kristen's favorite day of the week

This morning, the ICU Doctor sat us down to talk with us. She told us due to the uncontrollable bleeding and blood loss, that the replacement blood and plasma were artificial life support, it was only delaying the inevitable and prolonging her suffering. We decided at that time to discontinue the blood replenishment and let God do his thing.

We kept Kristen constantly informed of where Megan was on her journey home. Early in the morning she had left Orlando, was changing planes in Atlanta and arrived in Indy. Bill, a friend from church had picked Megan up and she was in the hospital parking lot. She walked into Kristen's room at noon.

Kristen had hung on for her sister to make it there and have an opportunity to say that she loved her. At 1:40 pm Kristen stepped through the doorway into eternal life with many friends and her family all around. Near the end, the ICU nurse, who only had met Kristen that morning, stepped over to a corner in the room and cried . . . . I got up and hugged her.

Over her lifetime especially the last 12 months Kristen had touched many lives, inspired many and loved many. Kristen, during this last year, fighting terminal cervical cancer, experiencing multiple surgeries and pain, hardly ever complained and was never afraid of the possible final outcome. She never lost hope, her sense of humor or the love she had for so many others. Her parents are very proud of her and we know God is too. We will miss her.

God has another new angel.

I'm not really here anymore
no opinion
no sharing
we order our death through windows
for our convenience

—Kristen

<u>June 6—Friday</u>

To everyone on our Kristen Update email lists:

On behalf of our entire family, Brenda, Eric, Megan and myself, I want to express our deepest thanks for being a part of Kristen's life for the last year. Your prayers have sustained us through this tough time. Kristen is free now, without pain . . . no more surgeries, no more chemo, no more radiation, no more 17 medications twice a day, no more wrapped legs, no more walker, wheelchair, no more bedside commode, no more ice packs, and no more colostomy. God has a new angel. I picture her sitting under a palm tree (her favorite) on a white sandy beach, listening to the waves break on to the shore. She is resting before God puts her to work caring for us.

The viewing on Wednesday and funeral on Thursday were incredible. Kristen was dressed with a T-shirt from Brenda's friend in Delaware that proudly said "One Brave Chick" on it . . . dedicated to those who have fought a major battle. Even the funeral director said "The viewing and celebration of her life was an impressive tribute to your daughter". Over 400, yes, 400 people signed her visitor's register. Our pastor even said this was one of the largest funerals he has ever done.

When we went out to the cemetery, the 75+ cars stopped traffic in Noblesville. My sister told me on the trip to the cemetery, she and Don were way back in the line of cars. Marcia said she was really amazed at all the cars and during the trip to the cemetery how all the police were stopping traffic at the key intersections. I told her the funeral home representative told us the contract included only one escort police officer. However, this policeman, on his own initiative, called two of his friends to help keep open the intersections. It was almost like he knew this was going to be a big one. But she said the most memorable part was that as they came along the route she noticed how people had not only pulled over, but some got out of their cars to stand and honor Kristen. Only a Princess could do that.

Last summer Eric brought Kristen beach sand from Florida, which she loved so much. He delivered the sand and an artificial palm tree to her room. She bragged about having the only hospital room with its own private beach. Yesterday at the cemetery, instead of sprinkling dirt on her coffin, everyone took some of the sand from Eric's summer gift and sprinkled it on her coffin along with her sea shells.

During the first surgery and hospital stay, Kristen awoke from a nap and looked at me with those beautiful blue eyes and said, "Dad, I am going to heaven". I was surprised at her statement and looked at her and said "I know . . . are you planning on leaving soon?" She said "No". I thought about that for a moment and said "Kristen, will you promise me something? Will you promise me that if you get there before I do, that you will stand at the gate and wait for me?" She smiled and said "Sure Dad, I will wait at the gate for you". I know my daughter is waiting at the gate for me!

A very grateful and proud Dad

Kristen M. Forbes, 23, Noblesville, passed away Sunday, June 1, 2008 at Riverview Hospital in Noblesville, IN. She was born November 15, 1984 in Indianapolis, Indiana to Brenda (Lindvall) and Kirk Forbes. Kristen worked for Walgreens as an Assistant Manager. She was a member of the Emmanuel United Methodist Church in Noblesville, Indiana. Kristen obtained a Business Management Degree from Indiana University, Kelley School of Business at Indianapolis. She was a lifetime member of the Girl Scouts, played cello in the Noblesville High School Orchestra, and was on the first Noblesville HS State Championship Women's Rugby team. She is survived by her parents, Kirk & Brenda Forbes of Noblesville; brother, Eric Forbes of Noblesville; sister, Megan Forbes of Orlando, FL; grandmother, Phyllis Lindvall of Culver, IN; many aunts, uncles, & cousins; best friends, Jeff Owens & Chelsea Sinsabaugh; family friend, Jamie Dye of Noblesville; and her best kitties, O.J. & Fiji.

Services will be held at 2:00 pm on Thursday, June 5, 2008 at Emmanuel United Methodist Church with a viewing at 1:00 pm. Family and friends may call Wednesday, June 4, 4:00-8:00 PM at Randall & Roberts Funeral Home, Noblesville. Burial will be at Crownland Cemetery in Noblesville. In lieu of flowers, memorial contributions may be made to the American Cancer Society—Relay For Life, Orlando, FL.

June 11—Wednesday

I arrived at Indianapolis Airport Signature FBO yesterday to pick up a plane. Everyone is wearing a wristband that says "Prevent and Detect Cervical Cancer" in honor of Kristen. Everyone came up to me and said how sorry they were. They sent us a card and donated money for cancer research and support. We think Kristen is going to raise well over $ 2,000 for the fight against cancer.

I told them, "We know she suffers no more and . . . . We will see her again someday!"

The Story Continues

In all my experiences, when I lost a loved one; Father, Mother, Grandparents, Father-In-Law, Step-Father, Aunts and Uncles, everything seems to pretty much follow the same road. We gather for the viewing, then burial at the cemetery, and topped off by a wonderful funeral meal back at the church. We share memories of good times and how much we will miss that person. Hugs, kisses, smiles and promises to meet more often than just at weddings and funerals. Accounts are transferred or closed, bills are paid and estates settled. Then, except for dealing with the grief, life goes on and most things return to normal.

But it was much different for us because . . . . Kristen's story continues . . .

— Dad

Jacob and Jeff checkout Kristen's final gift to them

Crumbs Left Behind

June 15—Sunday

One of the cute things about having small children . . . that I appreciate even more now . . . is when they leave a trail of crumbs behind them. You laugh as a parent, not realizing how important those times were until they grow up and leave you.

Well, Kristen has been leaving crumbs behind her. As we go through her things, we have found a Mother's Day card, which has now been delivered to Brenda, a thank you card to Megan for being with her last summer during her hospital stays and now delivered. Some gift cards for restaurants, which we have used in her celebration. All the happy party and vacation pictures on her computer. Eric reviewed them late one night and cried himself to sleep because he missed her so much.

I stopped at Walgreens yesterday to thank M, Kristen's pharmacist through all this. He smiled at me and said that Walgreens had their Cancer Relay for Life last weekend. He said they used Kristen (who was an Assistant Manager of Walgreens in Carmel) as a rallying cry and an example of how even an employee could benefit from the fund drive. He said they had a huge response. The best they have ever had. He credited the success to being able to make the focus more personal, and everyone knew Kristen.

We dismantled Kristen's wheelchair ramp, which Eric and I had built. We used the wood to make a sandbox for 5 yr old Jacob, whom she treated like a son. I built two corner seats and Brenda painted "Love, Kristen" on one. We are taking it to Jeff's house today to assemble and fill with sand. We stopped at the store and bought Jacob a bunch of sand toys.

Jeff is coming to our house tonight for supper and hanging out. We did the same with Chelsea, Kristen's other best friend, last week. We are trying to make a special effort to keep everyone glued together. It is especially tough on the younger adults, because they haven't had to face the death of a close friend. I told Chelsea that we have adopted her since her parents are in the process of relocating to Virginia this summer. Jeff said he feels like Eric is as close as a brother.

A crumb gathering and enjoying every minute of it.
Dad.

June 16—Monday

Megan has converted Kristen's MySpace website into a memorial site.

Kristen's MySpace is:

http://www.myspace.com/bestyouevahad

Megan also produced an excellent audiovisual presentation with photos and music for Kristen's funeral. A short version can be seen on YouTube at:

http://www.youtube.com/watch?v=4nE2UKerhbQ

The wonderful article written by friend Ward in the Zionsville Times Sentinel:

http://www.timessentinel.com/archivesearch/local_story_164172541.html

Just to let you know in addition to the more than 400 people who came and said goodbye to Kristen, we have received more than 160 cards and letters. All of them were wonderful!

Thank you so much.

A very proud Dad

July 6—Sunday

Yesterday we started cleaning out Kristen's storage unit and files. I found more crumbs. She had written a letter to herself five years ago when she was 18. It was an incredible eye opener. You will have to read it to understand. Kristen with her very profound and thoughtful writings, even in her journals she kept last year, is revealing a wonderful side of her I never saw. I knew she was special but now she is even more so.

Dad

May 21, 2003

Dear Kristen,

Think back to your senior year, I know it wasn't much, but can you remember that book? The book that made you question how you felt. The relationship you shared with the book, and how everyone else despised the book. The Bell Jar was like drinking water to you. But that is how good books come to you. The way you related so clearly to an insane person somewhat freaked you out. It made you feel different about everybody and your surroundings.

Back then you were satisfied with who you were. I'd say down to earth and how Andrew put it, "real". Dad always told you how caring and compassionate you were. I'm definitely still hoping you're like that. Do you remember the personal struggles, especially at the end of your senior year in high school? You showed such forgiveness; so much it could last a lifetime. I hope you made some good decisions, and where you are now is a safe place. I hope your heart has healed. Your individuality is something that is important to you. Knowing that you are still there means a lot, remember that. I worked hard to shape you. You better keep up the good work. I never made friends easily, considering our past. Just be careful, make friends with the right people. Don't let people be mean, stand up for yourself. Let them know you're an individual. Don't let others influence you. There was too much work that was put into you, for you to be ruined or stolen by people. Be the influence for others.

In high school Kristen just wanted to be free. Free from worry and stress of life. I doubt you're free from that. I want to be happy and to smile when I wake up. Are you there yet? I'm paying for college, so don't screw that up. Are you handling it okay when things aren't going well? Please remember that you have a very loving family. A family that will accept you no matter what you do. Remember that God is on your side. He will never give you more than what you can handle. Dad had said this is what life is, trials and temptations, no one ever said it would be easy. After a thunderstorm there is always a rainbow, even when you can't see it right away, there is one somewhere.

Don't forget what you have endured in life. Forgetting about it will not solve it. Carry it with you, your trials are a part of you. Stay strong and forgiving. Never give up on others that you love. We both know we wouldn't want them to give up on us. I don't know where our life stands now, but I pray that it is where God wants us to be.

This isn't a quote that will set life straight, but maybe it can remind you of Dad. "Don't ever forget to smile at people, even if your day is a bad day. The person that sees your smile might be just what they needed to see".

I hope Kristen, that you will remember my senior year and me. Also I hope you had a kick ass time in college!

Deepest love,

The 18 year old you,

Kristen Forbes

July 6—Sunday

Marcia,

Thanks again for the wonderful note, I really needed it. On Friday night we went to Conner Prairie Amphitheater to listen to the Indianapolis Symphony July 4th show and fireworks. It is a wonderful program and we try to do it every year. It didn't seem to be the same with the void Kristen left. Then yesterday we started cleaning out Kristen's storage unit and files. I knew she was special but now she is even more so. Unfortunately, the cleaning process left my heart ripe for a major hit.

Then last night we went to see a friend's daughter get married and I had to use all my energy to keep from crying. Oh, God this is so hard. When my friend's mom came up and gave me a hug, I had to fight to keep the tears in. I think going out on the road working is the only thing keeping me glued together right now.

Thanks for being a great Sis.

Kirk

July 7—Monday

Wow, what a special young lady. This has really touched me at how someone so young could be so wise beyond her years. I really take Kristen's letter to herself to heart being a parent of a little girl who is starting in her faith. What an inspiration. As proud as you are of Kristen, this must have just blown you away. You are wonderful parents and wonderful people and raised an absolutely loving, forgiving, and most importantly faithful daughter. I can only pray that I can raise my daughter to be the kind of inspiration that Kristen is and always will be.

A Friend

July 8—Tuesday

Several of you have asked how we are doing so I thought I would drop you a note. We are going back through all your cards and donations to fight cancer, which were given in Kristen's name and sending thank you cards. If we missed anyone, please know that your cards, letters and donations were wonderful.

I did well the first three weeks, probably because of the relief knowing Kristen suffered no more and the full time around-the-clock care was over. Then this last week I fell into a major funk . . . didn't quite know why I felt the way I did. Then a friend of mine, who many years ago lost a child, called and asked if I was carrying around a lump in my throat on the verge of crying. I said yes!!! He said I had the three week syndrome. He said anytime a friend loses someone they love, he marks his calendar and calls them at the 3-4 week mark, because that seems to be when they bottom out. I hope he is right, at least the call made me feel much better.

At the funeral many heard me tell about the wonderful things that had happened in the last year to Kristen and us. They told me I should write her story, so I started last week. If for nothing else, her little friend Jacob can someday read about how brave this young lady was and how much she loved him.

Someone gave us a card with the following on it.

I was moved at how true it is:

What Cancer Cannot Do

Cancer is so limited . . .

It cannot cripple Love
It cannot shatter Hope
It cannot corrode Faith
It cannot destroy Peace
It cannot kill Friendship
It cannot suppress Memories
It cannot silence Courage
It cannot invade the Soul
It cannot steal Eternal Life
It cannot conquer the Spirit

Author—Unknown

Kristen's Memorial Garden

July 9—Wednesday

More thanks to give:

Thanks to Karen for bringing us a pizza one night at the hospital. Others who brought flowers, gifts, visited, and shared money for expenses. I didn't realize how important hospital and home visits were until we were on the receiving end. I truly believe it helped maintain our strength and sanity for the entire year.

July 16—Wednesday

Back in February and March we encouraged Kristen to work on a garden. As she got weaker, she was only able to help start the seeds indoors. Eric and Mom watched over the seedlings for her and transplanted them into the garden. After she passed away, we decided that one way to keep her close and honor her was to have the garden become a memorial to her. At the funeral, a good friend gave us a stone angel for Kristen's garden. We placed it among the seedlings. Then a few weeks later they brought us a beautiful engraved memorial stone for the garden. We thought you would like to see photos of Kristen's Memorial Garden, the Angel and the Stone.

A very proud family
The Forbes

July 24—Thursday

We are going through more of Kristen's boxes and found the rest of her journals. In her 2003 journal, she describes how she wants her funeral:

February 4, 2003

My funeral

I want my funeral to happen on a sunny day. Spring preferably. And that all my friends, family, and coworkers come. I want pictures of my life everywhere along with beautiful flowers. I want people to cry, but then rejoice in my life and me joining the one who made me. I don't want people to dress in black, it's an ugly color. But I want them to wear colors. Afterwards, I want all my friends and family to have a party to celebrate my life."

She got all of it.

How profound.

July 24—Thursday

Today, the Forbes' are doing pretty well. We still have occasional meltdowns but they are the healthy ones. We had our first green beans last night from Kristen's Memorial Garden—Yum! The garden is going crazy. Our next door neighbor is on the "Neighborhood Tour of Gardens" and he said he was envious. Amazing what happens to a garden when a special angel is watching over it.

Last month Jeff, Eric and I dismantled Kristen's wheelchair ramp and converted it into a huge sandbox for Jacob. We assembled it and filled it with 1200 lbs of sand.

August 1—Friday

How many lives saved by sharing Kristen's story and encouraging young ladies to get the HPV vaccine?

October 11—Sunday

We were on vacation and I woke up at 3 am right in the middle of a dream. I started to cry. Brenda asked me what was wrong. In my dream God allowed me to go back a year, before this cancer journey began. Kristen was having a great time. But, all I could do was hold her close and cry, knowing what was ahead for her. She looked at me, smiled and couldn't figure out why I was so sad. I awoke still holding her.

* * * *

My Uncle Don said it best when I told him Kristen had passed away. He said, "Kirk, there is no way in the world, you could ever convince her to come back now." I told him, "I know . . . and I wouldn't want her back in the condition she was in."

But . . . it is so hard to say goodbye.
I know we will see her again.
She waits at the gate for us.
Love,

Dad, Mom, Megan & Eric

Dad's employer's wonderful gift—Kristen's Star

A Star is Born

My employer thought it a suitable tribute to look to the heavens, find a star and name it for Kristen, who now resides in the heavens with her star. The next time you look up on a clear night be sure to look to the southern sky. Locate the constellation Scorpius, then about half way down the body of the "Scorpion" and just west of the middle star. Look very close and you will see Star # TYC-7354-1051-1, which is now known as "Kristen" named by Kristen's supporters through the "Name A Star Live" program.

A Tribute From Her Family

I Remember . . . .

I remember when we would swim all summer long at the North Harbour pool and our blonde hair would turn green because of all the chlorine.

I remember when we used to put underwear on our heads and march around the house saying . . . "Hut, Hut, It's the underwear march!"

I remember when we used to build forts out of blankets and chairs in the living room.

I remember our sock wars. We would lie on the couch and throw our socks into the fan to try to hit each other.

I remember when you first got your glasses. They were big and round. We used to give you a hard time about them.

I remember when you got poison ivy at Girl Scout Day Camp. You had it everywhere . . . . and I mean everywhere.

I remember our parents spoiling us with the greatest family vacations.

I remember when our dad left us snorkeling in the ocean with the barracuda because Mom had gotten seasick.

I remember us riding in the outrigger canoe and you didn't have to paddle because you were the Princess.

I remember when we went SCUBA diving with the sea turtles in Hawaii.

I remember all the fun times we had on Morse Reservoir.

I remember when you came home with a ding in your car and told Dad that a tree jumped out in front of you.

I remember when you would drive me after school to the gas station to get blue raspberry slushies.

I remember when your rugby team won the first high school state championship.

I remember when you first got your dream car, a red Ford Mustang. You walked out to see it and said, "Dad, if this is a joke, it is not funny!"

I remember when you had a frozen water bottle thrown to you without you knowing and it hit you in the eye. You had to go to the emergency room and get stitches.

I remember how you loved Jacob like a son.

I remember how much you loved your kitties, Fiji and OJ.

12/21/2007

141

I remember you wanting to move to Florida after you graduated from college.

I remember how much you loved vacationing in Key West.

I remember how well you could play your guitar and cello.

I remember how much you loved listening to Jimmy Buffett and Dave Matthews.

I remember your love for palm trees and always telling me to hug them for you.

I remember how excited you were when you finally got your Nintendo Wii.

I remember our trip to Disney World last October with the Batch Family.

I remember when you were diagnosed with cancer and we weren't allowed to talk to you about it until the doctor did the following day. You called me in the morning and told me that you had cancer but you already knew that we were told the night before. I started crying and you told me to stop and everything would be ok.

I remember when you saw angels in your room.

I remember talking to you about how wonderful our parents have been over the past year.

I remember how excited you were every time you heard your big sister was coming home to see you.

I remember staying up all night coloring with you because we couldn't sleep.

I remember singing camp songs late at night with you in the hospital.

I remember watching movies with you into the early morning until you fell asleep.

I remember standing next to your bed the night before you passed and you reached out and grabbed my hand without looking for it.

I remember how you waited for your family and close friends to be with you before you went home.

I remember the high times and the low times.

I remember your love and compassion for others.

I remember your great personality and sense of humor.

I will always remember how wonderful of a sister you were.

A couple of nights ago Eric, Kristen's little brother, said he couldn't sleep in Kristen's room because "it smelled like Kristen" . . . . and then he cried. Suddenly it struck me . . . in 2nd Corinthians God says that Christians are "the fragrance of life" to those around them. From a father's perspective . . . what I saw of Kristen was good . . . not perfect . . . . but very good. I told Kristen that when we pass from this world, the only thing we leave behind are the lives we have touched. Everything else vanishes. It is obvious from looking around in the church this afternoon; Kristen has touched many, many lives.

Several people who have spoken to me, have been very distraught over "only 23 years" for Kristen. As we arranged the photos and shared Kristen stories that captured moments in her life, I realized that Kristen had packed more into her 23 years than most people do in two lifetimes. Growing up moments . . . . high school graduation, college business degree, participating in weddings, youth retreats and mission trips, scuba diving, sailing, fishing, rollercoaster riding, jet skiing, international traveling, Noblesville HS State Championship Rugby player, cello player in the orchestra, guitar player, nature lover, beach lover, parasailing, flying, swimmer, bowler, basketball, softball, gymnastics, Girl Scouts, YMCA Camp counselor, gardener, cat owner, substitute teacher, The Olde Custard Stand employee, Sinclair's Pizza employee, and assistant manager at Walgreen's.

Kristen's friend Ward once said that this life is only an audition for the "Real Life". I think Kristen has successfully completed her audition. Thank you God for sharing her with us.

Can you smell that wonderful aroma of life?

We can . . . . We will miss you Kristen . . . . enjoy your new life!

Hugging her favorite . . . a palm tree

I survive everyday
I'll do this till I die
I must
for that I'm forced
you wouldn't know
I look for understanding
but from who
and what reason
I close this book
with knowledge that
I've said what I said
no doubts
no regrets

—Kristen

Kristen's Wisdom, Poetry and Song

Wisdom, Poetry and Song

By Kristen Forbes

Throughout Kristen's life, she had a flair for journaling and writing poetry and song lyrics. I didn't know she even wrote poetry until we found two journals full of poetry. Surprisingly, she had been writing since she was 12 years old. Kristen told her Mom that one day she hoped her poems would be published. Here is a sampling of her creativity.

What do I enjoy the most
green grass and blue sky
these pages represent my
life so you should take that
into consideration while
you read what's inside
for what a person has inside is the most private
personal belonging one
may possess

Confused
from all
these
blank
pages

Take me
break me
prepare me Lord
For my life is yours
fill me
with your
Holy Spirit
Be kind to others you say
Late at night
I close my eyes to think of you
distractions will come tomorrow
I'm not ready for them
nor anything else

Word
beginning then to the end
If I can see clearly
why can't you friend
You put this up front
As a front of your own

Love, Kristen

Stupid people
bad habits
mix me numbers
for I'm next in line

152

How can anything be against me
the Lord is on my side
He is the way, the light, and the truth
never give up
keep hold of your faith
the Lord God is with you in time of great loss
do not turn away
the Lord shall carry you
stand firm on the faith of God
may I become your hands
and your precious feet O Lord
use me to do your work.

"Save your friends" they tell me
friends of mine, open your heart
oh Lord, how am I to reach them.
am I their only hope?
I pray for them.
save their souls.
do not let them perish,
but die with eternal life.

Finally cleansed
then chance to become dirty
more wanting then ever before
choice mine
choice made
feeling dirty
I feel the same
walking back on my own old path
my memories less pleasing than before
if pleasing was even a word to be used with this
for the demons have fallen and grace let in

Love, Kristen

Put in a box
loud loud
music
craziness runs through your bones
to the fingers
then you move
not knowing not caring

My gift with pen to be glorified
set and meant to free the world
have all the evil thoughts stop and think
not of themselves any longer
won't that be such a surprise

One long walk along a path
wandering through the green grass
roses all along these stairs
imagination fool
see it from my side

Left alone dreams
being greater
not of others but yourself
You're told this
and you do that
turn around and think
is it enough
and if not
or so
who is that enough for
do you live for yourself
someone else
or just kind of live
not my business of knowing
I just question the stubbornness
of everyday people

you and me

Who are you
half blinded through the mind
not for sight nor sound
could you look in the mirror and see through
or is it still your own reflection

Hatred is loved by emotional breakdowns
feared by ones own misunderstanding
not being accepted just shut out
and blown out of proportion

Left so unsatisfied
will you ever smile again
your eyes look in mine
empty answers fall behind

Black love
lightning striking

Love, Kristen

He's not going to heaven
oh barely alive
how can I teach him
with his stubbornness inside

My dreams unwilling
to be kept freely
such a difficult love
oh an unbalanced one
when done and over
strong and weak men will decide

Having thoughts of an unreal life
slowly kills me
I'm asking for more than you can give me
but I long for it
forgive me
I bow down to One
you ignore Him
why
minds on different matters compete
just push them aside and let me in

I guess I'll just write
my feelings down somewhere
pray for love
this world
I'm such a tired hand at ease
love shall not surrender
only let me rise up
to fall again

be true to yourself

Because I have such love for you
I'll rise up again
showing you how deep this love really goes
I'll ignore the torment I must go through
the rudeness, the hurtfulness
just for one sweet kiss of yours
indulge in me

Did I ever tell you
you're the love I have always been looking for
Praise God I found you
Lift his name
for you found him in the darkness
I cry because I am over filled with joy
How grace swept the thoughts of Christ
Do you understand what he did for all of us?
Still we are so unworthy, so full of hate and sin
But Blessed with the death of Christ
so we can see the Father
Rejoice and repent your sins
For the reward is great in Heaven
Make room Lord
your sheep are coming for eternal life.

I survive
everyday
I'll do this till I die
I must
for that I'm forced
you wouldn't know
I look for understanding
but from who
and what reason
I close this book
with knowledge that
I've said what I said
no doubts
no regrets

Sunshine
it's beautiful outside today
stress building
we all look everywhere
for relief
some of them are lucky
enough to find them
find sunshine
I want to see joy
taste happiness
dance around the room
with a SMILE
all over my face

You are told to live life to the fullest
would you die for Jesus
the reward is much better in Heaven
What reward can you find here to possess

Life is beautiful
fulfilling... never empty
only if you allow your eyes to open
all the way
so you can see the wonderful ways of people
the sunshine burns into my arm
skin baking in the sun
how the warmth spreads through
finger tips to my tiny toes
obligations are nothing
slip into our daily routine
slip into darkness
make everyday yours
make it fresh and exciting

Relaxing
just as the sun sets
then I find time
to come to terms with myself

The beat vibrates
touches my toes
shakes me into reality
something that
everyone can be touched by

Move back and forth
don't ask why
follow what you feel
and what you want to do
by day's end you'll feel
much better

Come with me
let me show you something
show you how the world is
wonderful

I enjoy when it rains early in the morning
nature sleeps in
to be like nature
free as the wind
maybe it should rain on someone
else's day
not this life
wishing days would pass by
but how hopeless
wishing life away
enjoyment
something someone may dream to enjoy

Everyone has left me
no more tears to hear me
now that you have stripped me
take the one thing
you haven't touched
my breath.

I'm not really here anymore
no opinion
no sharing
we order our death through windows
for our convenience

I fall into the same pattern everyday
unsure if I am keeping up with the
world around
all things pass by
but is it starting to fade too quickly

A dark moon lit sky
from a long drive
arriving peacefully
to fall beneath the clouds

Privacy is a virtue
so don't touch mine

Songs
expressions of twirled emotions

If you were born a second chance
would you live so you wouldn't fall short of
God's only glory or God's own eyes
would you change yourself
be any different from now
is this place really worth all the pain it
brings on

To have peace and love
maybe a peace from above
Lord forgive us all our sins
our selfish acts that win

walking swiftly upon the water
you tell me believe
don't be afraid you say
come with me

you are Christ the King
sent from above
we bow to your feet
for you are filled with love

let me make you a follower
grant you LIFE
you say I'll always love you
follow me in all my steps
so you can be free
love all around yourself
then come join me

For you can carry my cross upon your back
would it still matter, my reasons to pack
you so loved the world you gave your only son
are they yet ready, safe from the sins
you gave me water when I was dry
still you can give me life I deny
please give my soul a fire
one my heart desires

You can't survive when you're lonely
or with low self esteem
walking around looking for the
wrong thing doesn't help
love everyone
and let them know
faith helps us hold on
love keeps us going
find someone and give them
some sunshine
we all need a little
nothing matters until
mattering means nothing
want what you have
wishing gets you nowhere
things that happen today might
not be here tomorrow so
enjoy it
and celebrate

God so loved the world
that
He made people,
people
that could write of
their souls

Such words
that are so unexpressed
will this last
or is it just a simple test

I love making decisions
on my own
my thoughts
my soul
things work out the way
they should
unless time
becomes mixed up
thrown upside down
relief is coming
countdown
Sun rises and nose is
still in the books

The thoughts in my mind
were once so important that
I wrote them all down
I am such a machine now
being hurt too many times
and school
and work
I will never forget this feeling
it will help me be great

This is my prayer
my Thanksgiving
my plea for forgiveness
my cry for cleanness
forgive me Lord
for I have sinned
as all, some go unnoticed
I pray that the lost may be found
my words will leap from my mouth into your heart
hear them, also listen
do my will for this is your spot in the kingdom of heaven

I'm really excited
I can't tell you why
I feel comfort, belonging
almost fair breeze
all my worries in the world
can just float away
could possibly once
my mind rests at ease
yes.... exciting

Grandma Porter
(Written at 13 yrs. old)

She was the sweetest lady ever. She was the one who cooked your favorite meal and listened to what you had to say, respecting your opinion and helping you solve your problems.

Her and my Daddy's favorite topic to talk about was the stock market. What fun it was to listen to them! I have learned a lot ! It's like Grandma Porter passed down her kindness and wonderful knowledge to her only son, my Dad and now my Daddy is starting to pass all of that to me!! ☺ I love to learn about stuff, like caring for others. Now I am teaching my buddies.

The day my Grandma went home to heaven, I wrote a song.

Grandma, you have gone away today,
I don't know what to say
I don't know how to feel
I don't know how to deal
My head is full of emptiness
I do not wish to think of this
I know when I look into a mirror
You will not be there to hold me
To love me
To kiss me or to tell me that
Everything is going to be ok
At night as I look up to the sky
I talk to the stars as if it is you
And I am being heard
By your listening ears
The wind feels like your soft touch
Then I remember that it's just me
And the stars
No you
For you have gone away today
Gone away with God
Gone home
Home to Heaven

Dr. Darron Brown and the HPV Vaccine

INDIANAPOLIS, IN — Darron R. Brown, MD, Professor of Medicine Division of Infectious Diseases and Professor of Microbiology and Immunology at the Indiana University School of Medicine and a researcher with the Indiana University Simon Cancer Center, has been named a recipient of the 2009 PhRMA Clinical Trial Exceptional Service Award.

The award honors Dr. Brown's work as a researcher in the development of Gardasil, the Merck & Co. vaccine, against infection by the human papillomavirus, which can cause cervical cancer. Dr. Brown was a researcher involved in the development and clinical testing of Gardasil.

Biography

Dr. Brown received his M.D. at the University of Rochester School of Medicine and Dentistry, and completed his residency in medicine and fellowship in infectious diseases at the same institution. He joined the faculty at Indiana University School of Medicine in 1989 and received the Young Investigator Award in Virology from the Infectious Diseases Society of America in 1990. Dr. Brown is Professor of Medicine and Professor of Microbiology and Immunology. Dr. Brown's research focuses on the human papillomavirus (HPV), the causative agent of cervical cancer. He has published numerous papers on HPV pathogenesis, carcinogenesis, and epidemiology. Dr. Brown received the Tony and Mary Hulman Health Achievement Award for his work in developing an FDA-approved vaccine to prevent HPV and cervical cancer.

Scientist Helps Create World's First Cancer Vaccine

The World Health Organization reports that cervical cancer is the second leading cause of female cancer mortality worldwide, with about 288,000 deaths and 510,000 cases reported each year. In 2006, the FDA approved Gardasil for the prevention of cervical cancer caused by HPV types 16 and 18, which together cause approximately 75 percent of all cervical cancers worldwide.

Dr. Brown proved that the prototype HPV vaccine produced antibodies that could destroy the HPV virus. He helped lead the clinical study phase and first HPV vaccine trial in the world at Indiana University School of Medicine in 1996. Over the next decade, IU scientists conducted seven more vaccine trials with HPV, enrolling nearly 1,000 volunteers.

The proof of principle study, demonstrating effectiveness against HPV type 16 was published in 2002 in the New England Journal of Medicine with an editorial that asked, "The Beginning of the End for Cervical Cancer?" The answer is yes! The vaccine is a recombinant virus-like product that uses the exterior shell of HPV without any infectious viral components. The body believes the virus-like vaccine is the actual virus and initiates an immune response which prevents HPV infection.

The U.S. Food and Drug Administration approved the HPV vaccine, marketed under the brand name Gardasil by Merck & Co., in June 2006 for girls and women ages 9 to 26. Shortly thereafter, the Center for Disease Control and Prevention's Advisory Committee on Immunization Practices recommended that all girls ages 11 and 12 receive the vaccine. The vaccine has also been approved for boys and men.

"In my view, probably the most important contributions I made were during those early years, before we really believed we could actually start a vaccine trial with the HPV vaccine. Some of us had more faith than others that it could work, and admittedly I was skeptical. I think it was a lot of perseverance, stubbornness and passion on the part of people in my group, at Merck, and other many other institutions who really kept pushing until we got something that looked like it would work."—Dr. Brown.

The CDC reports about 10,000 new cases of cervical cancer each year in the U.S., with about 4,000 deaths. Dr. Brown says cervical cancer has a higher mortality rate than other cancers because treatments are not particularly effective, which emphases the critical importance of prevention against HPV. Gardasil offers the potential to save thousands of lives in the United States and elsewhere.

Research Interests

Dr. Brown's research interests in HPV are currently focused on the natural history of HPV infections, including early events such as virus transmission, immunologic response to infection, and duration of HPV detection. This includes later events such as low-level persistence, viral integration, and oncogenesis, epidemiology of HPV infections and HPV-associated cancers globally, and continued assessment of currently-available vaccines against HPV, as well as development of new prophylactic and therapeutic vaccines against HPV infection and disease.

Selected Publications

Hoffman K, Neeper M, Markus H, Brown D, Muller M, Jansen K. 1996. Sequence conservation within the major capsid protein of human papillomavirus (HPV) type 18 and formation of HPV 18 virus-like particles in *Saccharomyces cerevisiae*. J Gen Vir 77:465-468. Bryan J, Fife K, Pratt L, Jansen K, Brown D. 1997. Neutralization of human papillomavirus in the mouse xenograft system: correlation of neutralizing titer and ELISA titer against virus-like particles. J Med Virol 53:185-188.

Lowe R, Brown D, Cook J, George H, Hurni W, Joyce J, Lehman D, Markus M, Neeper M, Schultz L, Shaw A, Jansen K. 1997. Human papillomavirus type 11 (HPV 11) neutralizing antibody responses in the serum and genital mucosa of African green monkeys immunized with HPV 11 virus-like particles. J Infect Dis 176:1129-1134.

Yeager M, Aste-Amezaga M, Brown D, Martin M, Shah M, Cook J, Christensen N, Ackerson C, Lowe R, Smith P, Keller P and Jansen K. 2000. Neutralization of human papillomavirus pseudovirions: a novel and efficient approach to detect and characterize HPV neutralizing antibodies. Virology 278:570-577.

Brown D, Schroeder J, Robinson T, Bryan J, Barr E, Smith P, Suhr G, Fife K, Wheeler C, DiCello A, Chiacchierini L, and Jansen K. 2001.

Neutralization of HPV 11 by immune serum from VLP-vaccinated women: correlation with RIA titer. J Infect Diseases 184:1183-1186.

Koutsky L, Ault K, Wheeler C, Brown D, Barr E, Alverez F, Chiaccherini L, and Jansen K. 2002. Evaluation of an HPV type 16 virus-like particle vaccine in young women. New England J. Med. 347(21):1645-51.

Many thanks to Dr. Brown and all of his dedicated colleagues who are trying to prevent anymore Kristen experiences.

—The Forbes Family

Dr. Ian Frazer and the HPV Vaccine

Named Australian of the Year, Dr. Frazer has studied the human immune system for over 25 years. This led him to his fight against one of the leading causes of death in women on a global basis . . . . cervical cancer. Due to his dedication and medical breakthrough, women now have an opportunity for protection against this horrible disease. In his own words Dr. Frazer tells about HPV and the vaccine that is now available.

Dr. Ian Frazer, MD
Director, Diamantina Institute
Research Leader, Immunotherapy Group

Cervical cancer is, in many countries in the developing world, the most common cause of cancer death in women. This cancer, which kills at least quarter of a million women worldwide every year, generally develops in young adult life, though it can happen at any age. Cervical cancer is a rare consequence of persisting infection with an extremely common virus, human papillomavirus, spread through sexual activity. At least one in every three men and women will, sometime in their lifetime, catch a papillomavirus that can cause cervical cancer, though most of us get rid of it without ever knowing that we've had it. Because infection with these papillomaviruses is common, silent, and commonly persists for years, a single sexual contact can be enough to catch a virus that can start a cervical cancer. At the beginning, cervical cancer is a silent disease. However, through regular screening with pap smears, precancer and early cancer caused by persisting papillomavirus infection can usually be caught before it becomes a serious problem, and cured by surgery. Regular screening is essential, because the screening process is not perfect, and any single screening sample (Pap test) will only find cancer or precancer cells about half the time they're there. For women who can't clear papillomavirus infection themselves, progression from infection to precancer to cancer generally takes many years, so regular screening gives the best chance of catching any problem before it becomes serious. Unfortunately, there are no screening programs for cervical cancer in the developing world. When there are symptoms of cervical cancer, the disease is generally advanced, and often can't be cured. Women die of infections, of anaemia, or of kidney failure.

As every cervical cancer has a papillomavirus infection as its cause, it's perhaps the only cancer that we could eliminate entirely, by preventing infection with the relevant viruses. Fortunately we now have vaccines that trials have shown can prevent infection with the two papillomaviruses that most commonly cause cancer. These viruses together are responsible for about 70% of cervical cancer. The vaccines can prevent infection, and the consequent cancers, but they can't help to cure an existing infection. So, to be effective, they have to be given before the infection is caught. The best chance of that is if the vaccines are given before the start of sexual activity, as these viruses are usually caught sometime during the first 5-10 years after sexual activity starts. Because the vaccines are able to prevent only two of the viruses responsible for cervical cancer, they complement but are not a substitute for screening. The best chance of preventing cervical cancer is a combination of early vaccination and regular screening. The good news is that trials have shown that vaccination considerably reduces the chance that a screening test will show precancer or cancer requiring surgery. Our challenge is now to ensure that every woman worldwide is offered the opportunity of vaccination and screening, to minimise their risk of this all too common disease.

Biography

Dr. Ian Frazer was trained as a renal physician and clinical immunologist in Edinburgh, Scotland before immigrating in 1980 to Melbourne, Australia to pursue studies in viral immunology and autoimmunity at the Walter and Eliza Hall Institute of Medical Research with Prof Ian Mackay. In 1985 he moved to Brisbane to take up a teaching post with the University of Queensland, and he now holds a personal chair as head of the Diamantina Institute. Dr. Frazer holds research funding from several Australian and US funding bodies. He is a director of a biotechnology start-up company, Coridon, with an interest in optimizing and targeting polynucleotide vaccine protein expression. He is president of Cancer Council Australia, and advises the World Health Organization and the Bill and Melissa Gates Foundation on papillomavirus vaccines. He won the 2005 CSIRO Eureka Prize for Leadership in Science and the Australian of the Year in 2006. Dr. Frazer teaches immunology to undergraduate and graduate students of the University.

Research Interests

Dr. Frazer's current research interests include immunoregulation and immunotherapeutic vaccines for papillomavirus associated cancers.

Selected Publications

1. Frazer IH. (2004) "Prevention of cervical cancer through papillomavirus vaccination." **Nat Rev Immunol** 4(1):46-54.
2. Frazer IH, Quinn M, Nicklin JL, Tan J, Perrin LC, Ng P, et al. (2004) "Phase 1 study of HPV16-specific immunotherapy with E6E7 fusion protein and ISCOMATRIX (TM) adjuvant in women with cervical intraepithelial neoplasia." **Vaccine** 23(2):172-81.

The vaccine information is:

Proper Name: Human Papillomavirus Quadrivalent (Types 6, 11, 16, 18) Vaccine
Trade name: Gardasil ™
Manufacturer: Merck & Co. , Inc, License #0002

More information on this vaccine can be found at: www.fda.gov/cber/products/gardasil.htm

HPV Test & Vaccine Product Information

Until a few years ago the Pap test was the mainstay in the effort to battle cervical cancer. It is still a vital test which regularly needs to be in every woman's medical plan. So, ladies, if you haven't received a recent Pap test, please seek out your healthcare provider and schedule it soon.

In addition, recent medical research and technology discoveries have revealed that most cervical cancer and several other types of cancers are caused by the human papillomavirus HPV. This discovery opened the door for researchers to engineer new products to test for the presence of high risk strains of HPV and develop effective vaccines to prevent HPV infections. The following information are descriptions of some of the medical miracles available to you and your family.

HPV Detection Tests

cobas HPV™ Test—Roche

Product Name: cobas HPV Test™
Manufacturer: Roche Molecular Systems, Inc.

The cobas HPV (Human Papillomavirus) Test identifies women at highest risk for developing cervical cancer. This test will help physicians make early, more accurate decisions about patient care, which may prevent many women from developing this deadly disease. The cobas HPV Test is the only FDA-approved cervical cancer screening test that allows HPV 16 and 18 genotyping concurrently with high-risk HPV testing. It individually identifies genotypes 16 and 18, the two highest-risk HPV genotypes responsible for more than 70 percent of cervical cancer cases, while simultaneously detecting 12 other high risk HPV genotypes. The cobas HPV Test is an automated test run on the cobas 4800 system which is used to identify HPV DNA from 14 high risk genital HPV types that are commonly associated with cervical cancer. The test specifically identifies types HPV 16 and HPV 18 while concurrently detecting the rest of the high risk types (31, 33, 35, 39, 45, 51, 52, 56, 58, 59, 66 and 68). If test results are positive, the patient is likely infected with HPV.

FDA Reference:
http://www.accessdata.fda.gov/scripts/cdrh/cfdocs/cfTopic/pma/pma.cfm?num=P100020

The Digene HPV Test™—Digene Corporation

Product Name: Digene Hybrid Capture 2 High-Risk HPV DNA Test
Manufacturer: Digene Corporation

Qiagen's Digene HPV Test is the test approved by the U.S. Food and Drug Administration (FDA) that directly detects the presence of high-risk types of the HPV virus. When used along with a Pap to screen women 30 and older, it more accurately identifies who is at risk of developing cervical cancer than the Pap alone.

The Digene HC2 High-Risk HPV DNA Test is a laboratory test used to show the presence or absence of the genetic (DNA) material from the Human Papillomavirus (HPV), in cells from a woman's cervix. (The cervix is the lower part of the uterus or womb.) When HPV genetic material is found in these cells, it sometimes indicates the potential or the presence of disease. The cervical cells are usually obtained during a Pap Test ("pap smear"), when cells are obtained by gently scraping the surface of the cervix.

FDA Reference:
http://www.fda.gov/MedicalDevices/ProductsandMedicalProcedures/DeviceApprovalsandClearances/Recently-ApprovedDevices/ucm082556.htm

Cervista® HPV—Hologic, Inc.

Cervista HPV HR is the FDA-approved high-risk HPV test designed to detect all 14 oncogenic strains of HPV and reduce false-positive results associated with low-risk cross reactivity.

Product Name: Cervista™ HPV 16/18
Manufacturer: Hologic, Inc.

These reagents are used with the Invader Call ReporterTM software to identify DNA from human papillomavirus (HPV) types 16 and 18 in cervical samples. If test results are positive, the patient is likely to be infected with HPV type 16, 18 or both 16 and 18.

FDA Reference:
http://www.fda.gov/MedicalDevices/ProductsandMedicalProcedures/DeviceApprovalsandClearances/Recently-ApprovedDevices/ucm134061.htm

HPV Vaccines

Gardasil™

Proper Name: Human Papillomavirus Quadrivalent (Types 6, 11, 16, 18) Vaccine, Recombinant
Tradename: Gardasil ™
Manufacturer: Merck & Co. , Inc.

Indications:
Prevention of vulvar and vaginal cancer.

FDA Reference:
http://www.fda.gov/BiologicsBloodVaccines/Vaccines/ApprovedProducts/UCM094042

Cervarix™

Proper Name: Human Papillomavirus Bivalent (Types 16 and 18) Vaccine, Recombinant
Tradename: Cervarix
Manufacturer: GlaxoSmithKline Biologicals

Indications:
Prevention of cervical cancer, cervical intraepithelial neoplasia (CIN) grade 2 or worse and adenocarcinoma in situ, and cervical intraepithelial neoplasia (CIN) grade 1, caused by oncogenic human papillomavirus (HPV) types 16 and 18, in females 10 through 25 years of age.

FDA Reference:
http://www.fda.gov/MedicalDevices/ProductsandMedicalProcedures/
DeviceApprovalsandClearances/Recently-ApprovedDevices/ucm134061.
htm

The Kristen Forbes EVE Foundation

The Kristen Forbes EVE Foundation is a non-profit 501(c)(3) corporation based in Indiana.

Our Mission Statement

To support educational, vaccine and other healthcare programs to reduce the incidence of cervical cancer and HPV.

Our Vision

Cervical Cancer: ***Educate & Screen. Vaccinate. Eradicate.***

Why

A month after graduating from college, Kristen noticed her right ankle was starting to swell for no apparent reason. The idea for the Kristen Forbes EVE Foundation was born when Kirk and Brenda Forbes lost their 23 year old daughter Kristen Forbes after a year long battle with cervical cancer.

Visit our Website

- View our Foundation video at: http://vimeo.com/15494353
- Donate now to fight HPV & Cervical Cancer at: http://kristeneve. org/donate_now/

Kristen Forbes EVE Foundation, Inc.
www.kristeneve.org
kirkforbes@kristeneve.org

DONATE TO FIGHT HPV & CERVICAL CANCER

Prevention and Early Detection Saves Lives

Mission Statement

To help women, family members and caregivers battle the
personal issues related to cervical cancer and HPV
and
To advocate for cervical health in all women
by promoting prevention through education
about early vaccination, Pap testing regularly
and HPV testing when recommended.

The National Cervical Cancer Coalition (NCCC) Provides the following:

- A support network for cervical cancer patients and their families when faced with the difficulties of a cervical cancer diagnosis and persistent HPV disease.

- Development of multi-language educational materials focused on reaching underserved and uninsured women to improve access.

- A clearinghouse to provide cervical cancer information to organizations and the public with the latest information on cervical cancer disease.

WE NEED YOUR HELP. JOIN US TODAY.
MEMBERSHIP IS FREE.

Visit our Website at: www.nccc-online.org

Find out how you can help cervical cancer patients and their caregivers.
Help form a local chapter in your community.

National Cervical Cancer Coalition
HPV Cancer Coalition
6520 Platt Ave., #693
West Hills, CA 91307-3218
Hotline: 800.685.5531
Phone: 818.909.3849
www.nccc-online.org

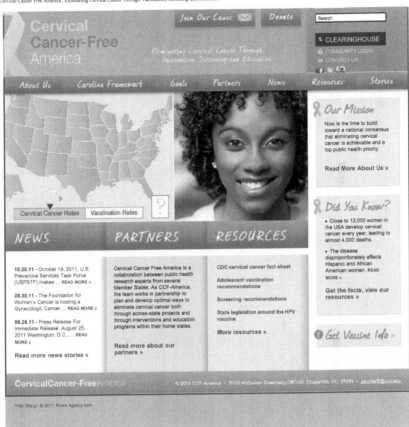

STAND UP TO CANCER™

An excerpt from this book is featured online at standup2cancer.org.

Stand Up To Cancer (SU2C) is a movement created to raise funds to accelerate groundbreaking research that will get new therapies to patients more quickly and save lives. All funds raised by SU2C are administered by the American Association for Cancer Research, the largest scientific organization in the world focusing on every aspect of high-quality, innovative cancer research.

SU2C is a program of the Entertainment Industry Foundation a 501(c)(3) charitable organization.

To learn how you can join the movement, visit su2c.org/getinvolved.

Resources

Kristen Forbes EVE Foundation, Inc.
www.kristeneve.org

Cervical Cancer-Free America
www.cervicalcancerfreeamerica.org

Relay for Life—American Cancer Society
1-800-ACS-2345 (1-800-227-2345) www.relayforlife.org/relay/

American Cancer Society
1-800-ACS-2345 (1-800-227-2345) www.cancer.org

Women's Cancer Network
Gynecologic Cancer Foundation
1-800-444-4441 www.wcn.org

National Cancer Institute
1-800-4-CANCER (1-800-422-6237) www.nci.nih.gov

Gynecologic Oncology Group
1-215-854-0770 www.gog.org

American Association for Cancer Research
1-866-423-3965 www.aacr.org

WordOnCancer
1-317-818-7668 www.wordoncancer.org

Epilogue

February 2012

It has been three and a half years since we said goodbye to Kristen. We miss Kristen very much—her beautiful blue eyes, wonderful smile, courage, deep faith and witty sense of humor. Yes, her absence leaves a huge void in our lives but we know that one day we will see her again.

Several friends have suggested I write a second book and recount all the amazing events that have occurred since Kristen passed away. In lieu of another book, allow me to reveal some of the blessings over the last three years in this epilogue.

My friend and fellow author Ward Degler reviewed the final version of **Love, Kristen** and convinced me to consider more than just handing out copies to our family and friends. He suggested an official book launch. We sold 250 copies that day and there are now over 1,100 copies in circulation. Midwest Book Review called it a "must read". **Love, Kristen** was named a Finalist in the Women's Issues category of the 2009 Next Generation Indie Book Awards. Kristen's story has been the subject of a Clinical Journal of Oncology Nursing Magazine article and a case study published for oncology professionals. A couple of universities are considering using the book to train their oncology nurses.

Because of the interest in HPV and its tie to cervical cancer, our book website (www.kristeneve.com) attracted 9,672 visitors from 82 countries in the first two years. While doing research for the book, I learned how little women knew about HPV and its tie to cervical cancer, the availability of new, safe and effective vaccines and the importance of HPV and Pap screening tests. I had the opportunity to do three TV interviews and a major radio station interview. Kristen's story was part of a nationally distributed Op-Ed/Press Release sent to most major TV, radio and print media across the nation.

The need to educate people about HPV and cervical cancer led us to create the Kristen Forbes EVE Foundation (www.kristeneve.org). While we were waiting for the IRS to approve the foundation's 501c3 application, I began reviewing HPV articles online to stay informed about new medical developments. I stumbled across an article in the University of North Carolina's campus newspaper about two researchers at UNC who had created the Cervical Cancer-Free America Initiative (www.cervicalcancerfreeamerica.org). At that time, this initiative involved only four states. I felt we should petition the group to include Indiana. To make a very long story short—after sending the initiative creators a letter, copies of *Love, Kristen*, several emails and finally a meeting in Chapel Hill, NC, they agreed to help Indiana become part of the Cervical Cancer-Free America program.

This development allowed us to create the Cervical Cancer-Free Indiana Initiative which focuses on education, prevention and screening. One of our goals is to educate specific target groups about the importance and effectiveness of HPV testing, HPV vaccination and cervical cancer screening. Our initiative is a collaboration of the Kristen Forbes EVE Foundation with the Indiana University Simon Cancer Center, Indiana State Department of Health, National Cervical Cancer Coalition and several corporate partners. Major supporters include the University of North Carolina's Gillings School of Global Public Health and the WORD on Cancer Foundation (www.wordoncancer.org).

In September 2010 WFYI and St. Vincent's Women's Health honored us for our efforts to improve women's health in Indiana. In December 2010 we received a generous grant from GlaxoSmithKline to begin the Cervical Cancer-Free Initiative in Indiana. Three months later in March 2011 we had a very successful Initiative Kickoff Meeting at Indiana University—Purdue University in Indianapolis with 135 attendees, including the Indiana State Department of Health, IU Simon Cancer Center, Indiana University School of Medicine, corporate personnel, various healthcare organizations and other collaborating foundations.

To our surprise, Kristen's story had personalized the disease and the battle cry of "no more Kristen experiences" was being heard more often. As 2011 progressed, more wonderful accomplishments occurred:

Indiana Governor Mitch Daniels issued a proclamation acknowledging a week in January as Indiana's Cervical Cancer Awareness Week.

The Indiana Female Legislators wrote a letter to the press announcing their support for the Cervical Cancer-Free Indiana Initiative and the Kristen Forbes EVE Foundation.

We created a Public Awareness Campaign to raise the visibility of HPV, the availability of effective vaccines, and cervical cancer screening by running 13,000—30 second spots on Comcast cable and 300,000 ad impressions on Comcast.net. In addition, we sent out Op-ed's to 275 media outlets in Indiana the first week of April including papers, magazines, radio and TV.

We joined the Indiana State Department of Health's Indiana Cancer Control Program, Office of Women's Health, Indiana Cancer Consortium and the Breast and Cervical Cancer Committee.

Along with our foundation website, we developed a social networking and marketing plan for the Cervical Cancer-Free Indiana Initiative using Facebook. We started the development of the Cervical Cancer-Free Indiana website which will become the premier source of information in Indiana for HPV and cervical cancer.

We participated in a college campus pilot project at Indiana University in Bloomington, IN. I gave a presentation to a class about cancer. In response they created a Vaccine Walk through campus to raise HPV awareness. This target audience was chosen because of the high infection rate of 45% for young women and men aged 20-24. They created T-shirts, a Facebook page, and chalked messages on campus sidewalks. We are planning on repeating this campaign at other college campuses in Indiana during the coming school years.

Our Foundation joined a coalition of eleven organizations in submitting joint testimony to a hearing at the Centers for Disease Control and Prevention (CDC) in support of routine HPV vaccination in males.

The Marion County Public Health Department created a PSA highlighting Kristen's story to stress the importance of the HPV vaccine for school age children. It will be shown throughout central Indiana.

Several corporations have indicated an interest in Kristen's story and the mission of the Kristen Forbes EVE Foundation. We are exploring major collaborations with companies interested in educating people about HPV and its tie to cervical cancer. In addition, we are inviting corporations with large employment bases in Indiana to become Cervical Cancer-Free companies.

In Indianapolis, we are planning to host a Midwest Regional HPV Conference for healthcare providers in Ohio, Kentucky, Illinois, Indiana and Michigan.

We are excited about what the future holds for Kristen's legacy and the Foundation's efforts to fight HPV and cervical cancer.

Thank you for all your support and prayers for the past three years.

The Forbes Family
February 2012

Notes

Note 1—CT Scan

A CT (Computerized Tomography) scanner is a type of X-ray machine. Instead of sending out a single X-ray through your body, several beams are sent simultaneously from different angles. The X-rays from the beams are detected after they have passed through the body and their strength is measured. A computer uses this information to present tissue density. The computer displays this as a two-dimensional image. CT scans help the doctors to see inside the body without having to operate and are helpful in diagnosing tumors.

Note 2—MRI

MRI (**M**agnetic **R**esonance **I**maging) uses magnetic and radio waves. There is no exposure to X-rays. The patient lies inside a large, cylinder-shaped magnet. Magnetic waves are sent through the body. This affects the body's atoms, forcing the nuclei to move. As they realign, they send out radio waves. The scanner picks up these waves and a computer turns them into an image.

Note 3—D & C Procedure

Dilation and Curettage—D&C

Curettage of the uterus (womb) is the scraping of the lining of the uterus. The procedure is commonly known as dilation and curettage or D&C. The main reason for performing a D&C is the investigation of a woman who is experiencing vaginal bleeding after menopause.

Note 4—PET Scan

A PET scan (**P**ositron **E**mission **T**opography) involves injecting a small dose of a sugar based, radioactive chemical, called a radiotracer, into the vein of your arm. The tracer travels through the body and is absorbed by the organs and tissues being studied. You will then lie down on a flat examination table that is moved into the center of a PET scanner—a doughnut-like shaped machine which shoots protons into the body to cause the IV fluid to glow and then map the areas of concentration. With the aid of a computer, this energy is converted into three-dimensional pictures.

Note 5—INR

International Normalization Ratio (INR) is the unit for reporting the clotting time of blood. A target INR level for a person taking anticoagulants is 2.0 to 3.0.

Note 6—PICC line

Peripherally **I**nserted **C**entral **C**atheter (PICC) is a form of intravenous access that can be used for up to a month.

Note 7—PowerPort

The **POWERPORT**™ device is a MRI-safe port which is surgically implanted for continuous IV, chemo or feeding (TPN).

Note 8—TPN

Total **P**arenteral **N**utrition (TPN) is a method to feed a person intravenously. The fluid includes water, amino acids, essential fatty acids, vitamins, minerals and electrolytes. All the basic needs to sustain life.

Note 9—Lymphedema

Lymphedema is the accumulation of lymph fluid in the fatty tissues below the skin surface, caused by a defect in the lymphatic system. Lymphedema is a frequent complication of cancer and its therapies, and can have long-term physical and psychosocial effects on patients. When the lymph system is damaged by either the cancer or the therapy it will not drain properly and the fluid buildup causes swelling. Breast cancer patients usually experience it in an arm or face. Cervical and ovarian patients experience it . . . in the legs and abdomen.